THE HOW AND WHY WONDER BOOK OF
AIRPLANES AND THE STORY OF FLIGHT

(Originally published under the title
The How and Why Wonder Book of Flight)

Written by HAROLD JOSEPH HIGHLAND, B.S., M.S., Ph.D.
Associate Professor, College of Business Administration,
Long Island University

Illustrated by GEORGE J. ZAFFO

Editorial Production: DONALD D. WOLF

ren's Museum, Brooklyn, New York

• Publishers • NEW YORK

Introduction

Scientists are filled with curiosity and this leads them to search for answers through exploration and experiment. This *How and Why Wonder Book* amply demonstrates how, over the years, the search for ways to move through the air has led to present-day miracles of flight. The book will help young scientists to widen their horizons of discovery about the unending efforts to conquer and explore space.

To fly like a bird has always been a hope of man. We know this from legend, mythology and recorded history. The hope has burned in man's dreams and challenged him to make the attempt. First it seemed like a dream of improbable fulfillment. Then gradually, from fumbling beginnings, success was achieved. Man flew! And now, in many ways, he flies better than the birds—higher and faster and beyond the air.

The How and Why Wonder Book of Airplanes and the Story of Flight helps the reader to relive the fascinating story of man's increasing mastery of the air from early attempts to present-day accomplishments. It takes the reader from the first flights of balloons, which merely drifted with the wind, to the *Apollo* moon missions. Here are answers to many questions about early types of planes, jets, missiles and rockets. Why does an airplane fly? What is the jet stream? How do pilots navigate in bad weather? And many others.

Everyone who is excited about living in the Space Age, at a time when man continues his effort to explore the solar system, should have this book of basic information about flight for reading and reference.

Paul E. Blackwood

Dr. Blackwood is a professional employee in the U. S. Office of Education. This book was edited by him in his private capacity and no official support or endorsement by the Office of Education is intended or should be inferred.

Library of Congress Catalog Card No.: 73-124652
(Originally published under the title
The How and Why Wonder Book of Flight)

ISBN: 0-448-05065-X (Wonder Book Edition)
ISBN: 0-448-04018-2 (Trade Edition)
ISBN: 0-448-03815-3 (Library Edition)

1983 PRINTING
Copyright © 1961, 1967, 1969, 1970, 1971, 1975, by Grosset & Dunlap, Inc.
All rights reserved under International and Pan-American Copyright Conventions.
Published simultaneously in Canada.   Printed in the United States of America.

Contents

Man gave the power of flight to gods and sacred animals. The winged bull is an Assyrian sculpture of the ninth century B.C.

The sphinx, a symbol of Egyptian royalty, was adopted by the Greeks. But it was given wings and served as tomb sculpture in the sixth century B.C.

This detail from a Greek vase of the fourth century B.C. shows the mythical hero Bellerophon mounted on his winged horse Pegasus. Together, they slew the dreaded Chimera. Sculptures similar to these are exhibited at the Metropolitan Museum of Art, New York.

Dreams of Flight

The story of man's dream of flight, of his desire to reach the stars, is as old as mankind itself. It is easy to imagine that prehistoric man, faced with a fierce, attacking monster, yearned to spring up and fly away just like a bird.

In ancient folklore and religions, we have ample proof of this desire to fly. But desires and dreams cannot lift a man off the earth, and so the wondrous ability to fly was reserved for his gods. Each of the gods had some means of flight. In ancient Greece, Phaeton, son of Helios, the sun god, drove the wild horses that pulled the sun chariot. Mercury, the messenger of the gods, had a winged helmet and winged sandals. The

Out of man's ancient dream of flight came this extension of his desire — a winged lion (Middle Ages).

The woodcut by the German painter and engraver, Albrecht Dürer, depicts Daedalus and Icarus fleeing the island of Crete. But Icarus perished in the sea.

winged horse, Pegasus, was able to fly faster, farther and higher than any bird.

The dream of flight was universal. In ancient Egypt and Babylonia, they pictured winged bulls, winged lions and even men with wings. The ancient Chinese, Greeks, Aztecs of Central America, Iroquois of North America, all shared this dream.

According to Greek legend, Daedalus,

Who was the first man to fly?

the Athenian inventor, was the first man to fly. He and his son, Icarus, had been imprisoned on the island of Crete by King Minos. In order to escape, Daedalus shaped wings of wax into which he stuck bird feathers.

During their flight, Icarus flew too high and the sun melted the wax. He was drowned in the sea, and that body of water is still called the Icarian Sea in honor of the first man to lose his life in flying. The father is supposed to have continued his flight and reached Sicily, several hundred miles away.

There is also an English legend of King Bladud who, during his reign in the ninth century B.C., used wings to fly. But his flight was short-lived and he fell to his death.

The dream of flying continued, but in all the legends, the flier rose like a bird only to fall like a stone. It was more than twenty-six hundred years after King Bladud's flight that men flew up into the air and returned to earth safely.

The first man to approach flying on a

What is ethereal air?

scientific basis was Roger Bacon, an Englishman who lived during the thirteenth century. He envisioned the air about us as a sea, and he believed that a balloon could float on the air just as a boat did on water. His balloon, or air boat, was to be filled with *ethereal air* so that it might float on the air sea. We do not know what Bacon meant by ethereal air; yet, many still credit him with the basic concept of balloon flight.

Almost four hundred years later, Francesco de Lana, an Italian priest, applied Bacon's principle of air flight. He designed a boat, complete with mast

A Frenchman named Besnier claimed that he flew the above contraption in the late seventeenth century.

De Lana's air boat was held aloft by four spheres.

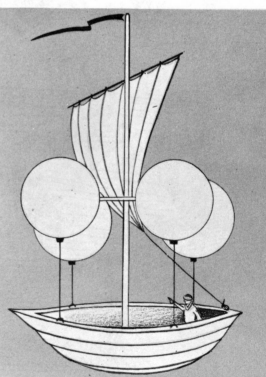

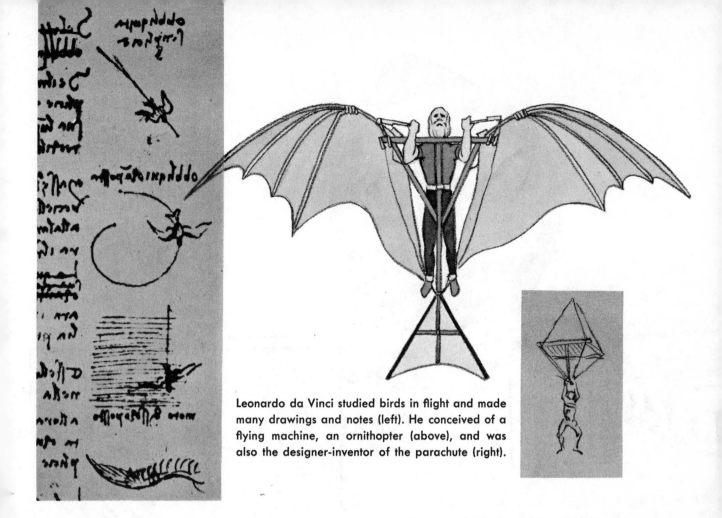

Leonardo da Vinci studied birds in flight and made many drawings and notes (left). He conceived of a flying machine, an ornithopter (above), and was also the designer-inventor of the parachute (right).

and sail, which would be held in the air by four hollow spheres. Each of the four balls was to be 20 feet in diameter and made of very thin copper. The air was to be removed from the balls so that they could float in the sky and lift the boat into the air.

De Lana's boat was never built since it was not possible to make spheres of such thin metal and such size in those days. Even if they had been built, the thin spheres would have been crushed by the pressure of the atmosphere.

Leonardo da Vinci was not only the greatest mathematician of the fifteenth century, but also a noted painter, architect, sculptor, engineer and musician. After studying the flight of birds and the movement of the air,

What is an ornithopter?

he reasoned that birds flew because they flapped their wings and that it was possible for man to do the same. Da Vinci designed the *ornithopter* (or-ni-THOP-ter), a flapping-wing flying machine. The wings were to be moved by a man's arms and legs.

Ornithopters were tried by many men. Robert Hooke experimented with this means of flight in England about 1650. He claimed he succeeded in flying, but he also wrote of his great difficulties to remain in the air. He is the first man who recognized that feathers were not needed for flight.

Many men tried and failed to fly with the ornithopter. It was not until 1890 that Octave Chanute discovered why this method would never succeed — man could not develop sufficient power with only his arms and legs.

The first balloon flights were made in 1783 when the Montgolfier brothers used heated air to make an ornate balloon rise.

One of the memorable early balloon flights was made by J. A. C. Charles, a French physicist, and one of the Robert brothers. The flight lasted over two hours, reaching a two-mile height.

The Age of Aerostatics

How did aerostatics help man to fly?

In 1643, Evangelista Torricelli demonstrated that the earth's atmosphere is more than just empty space. With his barometer, he proved that the atmosphere has weight and density, just like any gas. This discovery was the beginning of the science of *aerostatics*. Aerostatics (aero-STAT-ics) is the study of how an object is supported in the air by buoyancy; that is, its ability to float in air as a boat floats on water.

A milestone in this new science was reached ten years before the Declaration of Independence. Henry Cavendish, an English scientist, mixed iron, tin and zinc shavings with oil of vitriol and discovered a new gas which was lighter than air. Cavendish's "inflammable air" was later named "hydrogen" by the French chemist, Lavoisier.

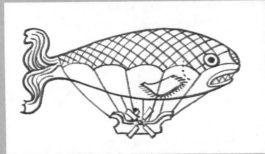

This fishlike flying contraption was constructed in France in the early 1800's, but it never flew.

This is typical of the early modern balloons, which were less ornate than the previous ones.

How did the first balloonists fly?

Some sixteen years after Cavendish discovered his new gas, Joseph and Jacques Montgolfier, French ornithoptists, were fascinated by watching smoke travel up from the fireplace through the chimney. They conceived the idea of making a smoke cloud which would fly in the air. They took a lightweight bag, filled it with smoke, and watched it float through the air.

After numerous experiments, they made a large linen bag, about 110 feet in circumference. At Annonay, in June, 1783, they had the bag suspended over a pan of burning charcoal in order to fill it with smoke. The smoke-filled bag rose almost 6,000 feet into the air and stayed aloft for ten minutes. It fell to earth a couple of miles away as the heated gas eventually cooled. A man-made object had actually flown.

With the French Royal Academy of Sciences, the brothers built a larger balloon, 41 feet in diameter. It carried

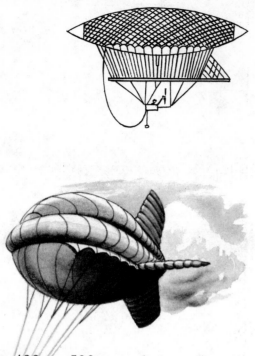

Henri Giffard built the first successful dirigible (top left) in 1852. It was powered by a propeller driven by a steam engine. The first controllable dirigible (above) was built by Alberto Santos-Dumont. Barrage balloons (left) were used in World Wars I and II to prevent low-level flying attacks by enemy planes.

some 400 to 500 pounds into the air, thus proving that it was possible to lift a man. On September 19, 1783, the new balloon carried its first passengers — a duck, a rooster and a sheep, and returned them safely to earth. Less than one month later, the first human ascent was made. Jean Francois Pilâtre de Rozier stayed aloft for over 4 minutes and reached a height of almost 85 feet.

Shortly after Pilâtre de Rozier took the

Why did the hydrogen balloon fly? first balloon flight, J. A. C. Charles, a French physicist, filled a rubber-coated silk balloon with hydrogen, which Cavendish had discovered. This balloon rose more rapidly than the earlier ones, remained in flight for almost 45 minutes, and landed over 16 miles away. Professor Charles raced after the balloon, but when he arrived he found the peasants using pitchforks to kill the unknown "monster."

The *Charlière,* as hydrogen balloons were called for many years, rose rapidly because hydrogen is considerably lighter than smoke or air. The weight of the air in a balloon that is about 3½ feet in diameter is 8 pounds. The weight of hydrogen in a similar balloon is only ½ pound.

The greatest of the early balloonists was

Who were other famous early balloonists? Francois Blanchard, who demonstrated balloon flying all over Europe and made the first American balloon flight on January 9, 1793. His most famous flight was across the English Channel in 1785, when he established the first international air mail on record.

Another famous early balloonist was Captain Coutelle of the French Revolutionary Army, who manned the first

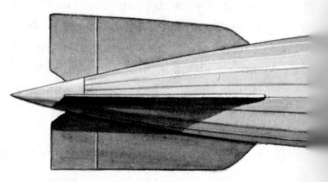

The zeppelin had a metal frame in which "bags" of hydrogen were used to make the craft "float."

balloon used in warfare. In 1794, at the battle of Fleurus, the captain signaled information to General Jourdan, who was able to take advantage of the shifting battle situation and emerged victorious.

The early balloons consisted of an inflated bag to which an open basket, or *gondola* (GON-do-la), was attached by ropes. To

How does a dirigible differ from a balloon?

make the balloon go higher into the air, the "pilot" lightened its weight by dropping bags of sand, which were secured to the sides of the gondola. To make the balloon descend, he opened a valve and let some of the gas escape. The balloon rose into the air, but there was no way to control its flight. Once aloft, the balloon — and the men with it — were at the mercy of the winds.

The *dirigible* (DIR-i-gi-ble), or airship as it is sometimes called, can be steered. It consists of an elongated, gasfilled bag with cars, or gondolas, below for passengers and power. The dirigible takes advantage of the wind, but also uses motor-driven propellers. The early dirigibles used a sliding weight to make them go up or down. Pushing the weight toward the front pointed the nose of the airship down; conversely, with the weight toward the back, the nose pointed upward. Later dirigibles used horizontal tail fins to direct their upward and downward movement. Vertical tail fins were used to steer them right and left.

In 1852, almost seventy years after the first Montgolfier balloon rose over Annonay, a

When did the first dirigible fly?

French engineer, Henri Giffard, built the first successful dirigible. Shaped like a cigar, it was 143 feet long and was powered by a 3-horsepower steam engine with a propeller attached to the gondola. Because of its low speed, about six miles per hour, this airship was pushed backward in a strong wind.

The first dirigible which could be accurately controlled and guided was *Airship Number One,* built by Alberto Santos-Dumont, a Brazilian millionaire living in France. In 1901, he flew his airship around the Eiffel Tower in Paris.

The early dirigibles were nonrigid; that is, they were long gasfilled bags. A gondola and powered propeller

What is a zeppelin?

were attached. When longitudinal framing, running the length of the bag, was used as reinforcement, the semi-rigid dirigible was created.

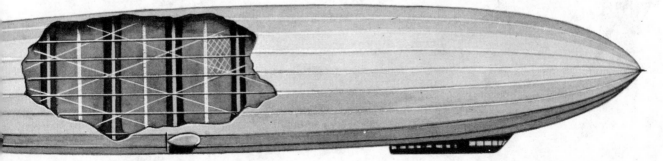

PLANES OF WORLD WAR I

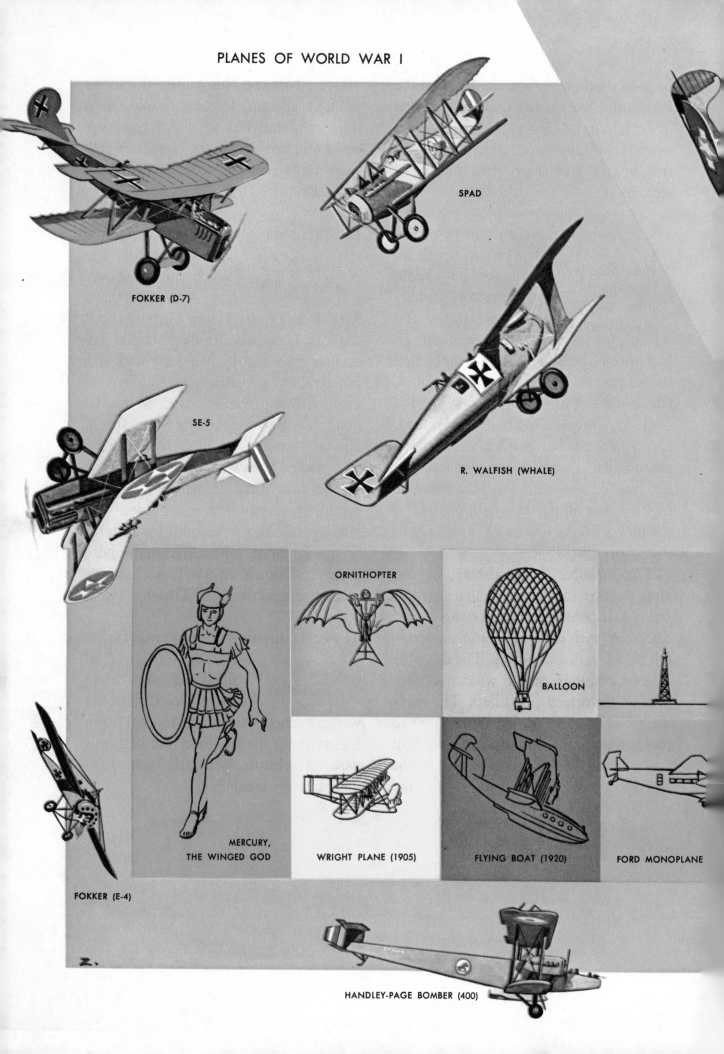

FOKKER (D-7)

SPAD

R. WALFISH (WHALE)

SE-5

ORNITHOPTER

BALLOON

MERCURY,
THE WINGED GOD

WRIGHT PLANE (1905)

FLYING BOAT (1920)

FORD MONOPLANE

FOKKER (E-4)

HANDLEY-PAGE BOMBER (400)

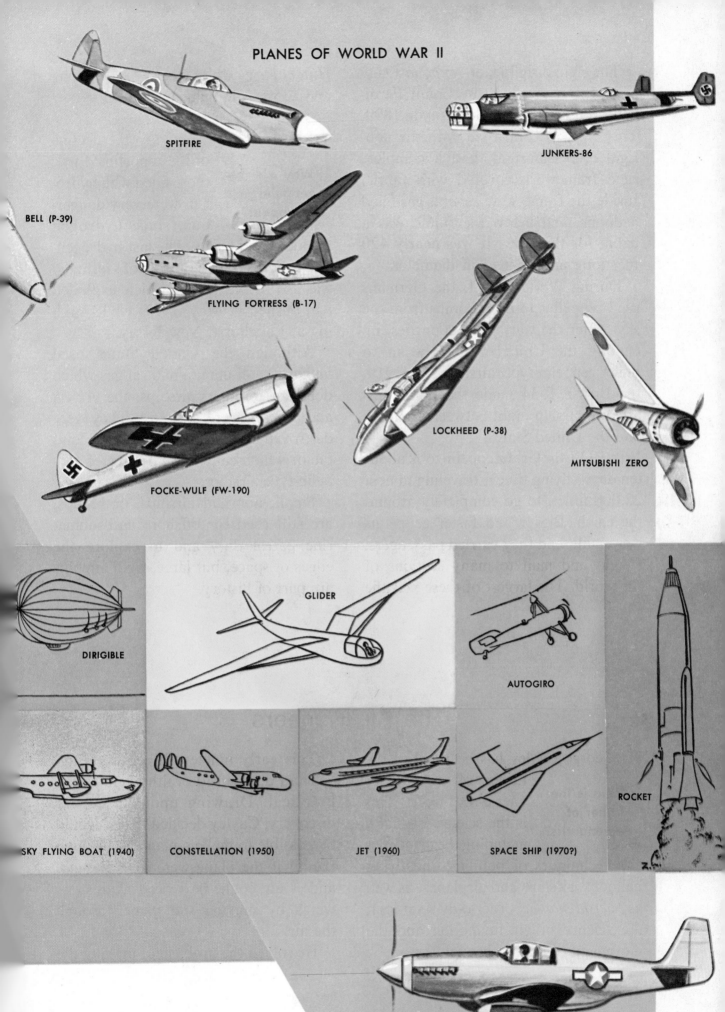

PLANES OF WORLD WAR II

SPITFIRE

JUNKERS-86

BELL (P-39)

FLYING FORTRESS (B-17)

LOCKHEED (P-38)

MITSUBISHI ZERO

FOCKE-WULF (FW-190)

DIRIGIBLE

GLIDER

AUTOGIRO

ROCKET

SKY FLYING BOAT (1940)

CONSTELLATION (1950)

JET (1960)

SPACE SHIP (1970?)

MUSTANG (P-51)

The rigid dirigible, or *zeppelin* (ZEP-pe-lin), was first built by Count Ferdinand von Zeppelin of Germany in 1899. This type, as contrasted with the non-rigid and semi-rigid, had a complete rigid framework covered with fabric. Inside the frame were several gas-filled balloons, and below the frame was a cabin for the crew. It was nearly 420 feet long and 38 feet in diameter.

During World War I, the Germans used zeppelins to drop bombs from the sky. After the war, other countries, including the United States, began to build zeppelin-type airships. In 1919, the British R-34 made the first transatlantic airship flight between England and the United States.

In 1929, the Graf Zeppelin took about ten days (flying time), traveling almost 22,000 miles, to go completely around the earth. Bigger and faster zeppelins were built, and they carried passengers, freight and mail to many sections of the world. The largest of these was the *Hindenburg,* which was 812 feet long and 135 feet in diameter.

Why did the zeppelin disappear? Two factors contributed to the decline of the zeppelins. First, those filled with hydrogen were very dangerous, since hydrogen explodes and burns. The last hydrogen-filled zeppelin seen outside of Germany was the *Hindenburg,* which exploded and burned in May, 1937, while landing at Lakehurst, New Jersey.

Although the United States used *helium* (HE-li-um), a natural gas which does not burn, its airships, the *Akron* and *Macon,* were both lost. They were destroyed by bad weather, the second factor which caused the decline of zeppelin-type airships.

Small, nonrigid airships, or blimps, are still used for offshore anti-submarine patrol duty and to explore the edges of space, but large, rigid airships are part of history.

The Air Pioneers

Who is the father of aeronautics? Sir George Cayley has been called the father of *aeronautics* (aer-o-NAU-tics). This is the science of flight, including the principles and techniques of building and flying balloons, airships and airplanes, as well as *aerodynamics* (aer-o-dy-NAM-ics), the science of air in motion and the movement of bodies through the air.

This early nineteenth century Englishman denounced ornithopters as impractical. Drawing upon an earlier discovery, Cayley decided that it would be possible to make a plane fly through the air if the plane were light enough, and if air could be forced against its wings by moving the plane through the air.

He solved the problem of making the

plane light by using diagonal bracing to reinforce the wings and body instead of using solid pieces of wood. The second problem, moving the ship through the air, was to be solved by a propeller-driven engine. Since there was no engine light enough or powerful enough, Cayley designed his own. It was an internal combustion engine which would use "oil of tar," or gasoline, as we now call it. But the fuel was too costly and Cayley was forced to abandon his engine. It was not until almost a hundred years later that such an engine was successfully built.

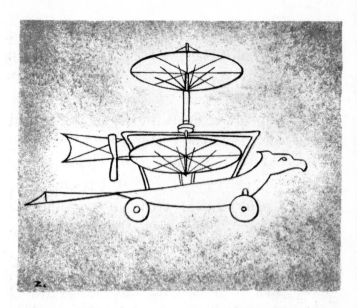

Sir George Cayley, father of aeronautics, built a successful glider in 1804, but he was unable to build a powered aircraft. His designs, however, were good.

Powered flight really started with William Henson and John Stringfellow. Using Cayley's principles, these two

When did the first powered airplane fly?

Englishmen designed an *aerial steam carriage* in 1842. Many of their ideas were practical, but they, too, were ahead of their time — there was no adequate engine.

In 1848, Stringfellow, working alone, built a model 10 feet long with a batlike wing. It had an engine which weighed less than 9 pounds and powered two propellers. It made short, sustained flights, flying as much as 40 yards. It was only a model, but it was real, powered flight.

The immediate ancestor of the successful powered airplane was the glider. It is a heavier-than-air ma-

How does a glider fly?

chine *without* an engine. The glider uses air currents to sustain its flight. In calm weather, it can be launched

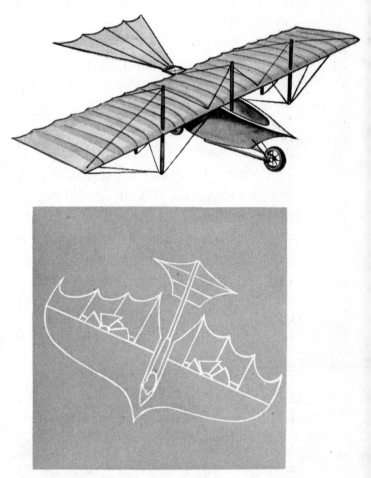

Powered flight came closer to reality with William Samuel Henson and John Stringfellow. They designed and flew the first powered models. But they were unable to build an engine to power a full-size plane.

from a high hilltop to obtain the needed forward thrust. The air rushing past its wings creates the necessary upward lift to counteract the gravitational force. The glider floats on the air and gradually descends to the ground.

In strong winds, the glider can be launched uphill so that it is picked up by the strong currents. It soars into the sky and continues to fly until the wind currents can no longer sustain it.

The greatest contribution in this field was made by Otto and Gustav Lilienthal. While still in high school in Germany, Otto built his first glider. It had wings that measured 6 by 3 feet each. In 1891, in Anklam, Germany, Otto made the first successful glider flight.

The brothers, noticing that birds took off *into* the wind, did the same with their gliders. They built many monoplane (single wing) and biplane (double wing) gliders and made over two thousand successful flights.

Perhaps Otto Lilienthal could have flown an airplane if a successful engine were available. In his attempt to develop such an engine, Otto lost his life. His experimental engine failed in flight and the airplane crashed.

Who made the first successful powered flight? Professor Langley, mathematician, physicist and Director of the Smithsonian Institution in Washington, D. C., was the last great air pioneer who failed to fly a plane. Using models, he supplied the answers to several problems which had to be solved before flying could be successful.

Early in the Spanish-American War, President McKinley asked Langley to develop a flying machine. Langley's assistant, Charles Manly, designed and built the first radial engine — the cylinders are built in a circle around the crankshaft. The engine used gasoline as fuel — it was Cayley's dream come true, almost a hundred years later.

Langley's *aerodrome* (AER-o-drome), as he called his plane, failed to fly on its second test on October 7, 1903. But some two months later, on December 17, 1903, at Kitty Hawk, North Carolina, the Wright brothers made the first successful flight.

Wilbur and Orville Wright were bicycle manufacturers from Dayton, Ohio, who built and flew gliders as early as 1900. After extensive work

The brothers Otto and Gustav Lilienthal paved the way for modern aviation. They built many gliders which flew successfully, and attempted powered flight. Otto was killed while testing a glider to which was attached a motor run by carbon dioxide.

on models, tested in wind tunnels, the Wright brothers designed and built their engine — a 4-cylinder model, weighing about 200 pounds, which developed 12 horsepower. They mounted this engine in a reinforced glider, and at Kitty Hawk, Orville Wright made four successful flights in one day. The first lasted only 12 seconds during which time the plane flew 120 feet. On the fourth flight the plane covered 852 feet and remained in the air for 59 seconds.

Despite its advanced engine, Samuel Langley's plane failed to fly. The gasoline engine, weighing less than three pounds per horsepower, was unequaled for twenty years.

The Wright brothers worked in Dayton for five years after their success at Kitty Hawk. In 1908, they developed a military airplane for the U. S. Army and in 1909, they demonstrated that a plane was capable of carrying a passenger. It flew at 40 miles per hour, carrying enough gasoline for a flight of 125 miles.

How did early aviation progress?

All over Europe and America, successful airplanes were demonstrated. In 1909, Louis Blériot flew across the English Channel. In that same year, the first international air meet was held at Rheims, France with thirty-eight airplanes participating. At that meet, Glenn H. Curtiss, an airplane designer and builder from the United States, established a speed record of 47.8 miles per hour. Hubert Latham set an altitude record of 508 feet, while Henri Farman, a Frenchman, established the endurance record of 3 hours and 5 minutes. The

17

On December 17, 1903, at Kitty Hawk, North Carolina, the first heavier-than-air plane was flown by the Wrights.

Louis Blériot set a new record when, in 1909, he flew across the English Channel in this small plane.

The first plane to take off and land on a ship at sea was flown by Eugene Ely, an American (1910).

Glenn Curtis was not only a plane designer and pilot, but also a manufacturer.

longest flight at the meet was 118 miles.

One year later, in 1910, Eugene Ely, an American pilot, demonstrated a flight which eventually led to aircraft carriers. His plane took off from the cruiser *U.S.S. Birmingham* and landed on the battleship *U.S.S. Pennsylvania*.

The outbreak of World War I spurred the development of the airplane. Although attention was concentrated on the plane as a military weapon, it helped to establish aviation, train pilots, foster aircraft manufacturing and increase the public's awareness of aviation's possibilities.

Many men took to flying. They bought surplus Government airplanes, and earned their living doing stunt flying and taking people up for short flights around airports. These men were the so-called "gypsies" and "barnstormers" who helped aviation to grow.

The NC-4 prove 1919, that a ocean expanse not limit travel b

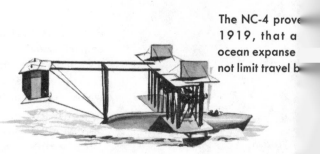

In May 1919, the NC-4 made aviation

How did airplanes "shrink" the world?

history by crossing the Atlantic. The Navy had three patrol bombers, flying boats which could take off and land only in water. Each plane carried a crew of six. Only the NC-4 completed the journey from Rockaway, Long Island to Plymouth, England, a distance of 3,925 miles. Some fifty destroyers lined the Atlantic to act as guides for the planes and to be ready to help any that were in distress. The total flying time was 52½ hours, not including the time necessary at the seven stops for refueling and repairs.

In 1924, the Army sent its Douglas biplane bombers on a flight around the world. Four planes left Seattle, Washington on April 6. On September 28, only two — the *Chicago* and the *New Orleans* — returned. They had crossed twenty-eight countries, covered 26,345

Some 33 hours and 30 minutes after he took off from Roosevelt Field in Long Island, Lindbergh landed his *Spirit of St. Louis* at Le Bourget, an airfield outside of Paris.

Two Douglas World Cruisers carried their Army flight crews in the first round-the-world flight in 1924.

During parts of their trip, the landing wheels were replaced by pontoons.

miles, and crossed the Pacific for the first time. The actual flying time was about 15½ days.

The race from New York to Paris was

Who made the first nonstop solo flight across the Atlantic?

spurred by a $25,000 prize which Raymond Orteig, French-born owner of a New York hotel, offered to the first one to make the flight nonstop. Although Orteig offered this money in 1919, it was not until 1926 that Rene Founck, a famous French aviator of World War I, made the first try. His plane crashed at take-off.

Many others tried and failed. It was Captain Charles A. Lindbergh, a former mail pilot, Army officer and barnstormer, who finally claimed the prize. Financed by a group of St. Louis businessmen, Lindbergh had Ryan Aircraft of San Diego build a special monoplane with a Wright J-5 Whirlwind engine at a cost of $10,580. The builders at Ryan worked as many as eighteen hours a day to complete the plane in sixty days.

Lindbergh brought his plane, *The Spirit of St. Louis,* to Roosevelt Field, Long Island where, despite the fog and drizzle, he took off at 7:52 A.M. on May 20, 1927. To make room for extra gasoline, Lindbergh flew alone. To make the plane lighter, he carried no parachute and removed the radio and all other "surplus" equipment and charts.

Alone, with no radio, Lindbergh plowed through rain, sleet, fog and high winds across the Atlantic, flew over Ireland and England and on over France. He circled the Eiffel Tower and landed nearby at the airport of Le Bourget, on May 21 at 10:22 P.M., Paris time. He had flown over 3,600 miles in 33 hours and 30 minutes.

The "Lone Eagle," as Lindbergh was called, was greeted by large, enthusiastic crowds. He received wild welcomes everywhere he went. The world was talking about "Lucky Lindy" — and aviation.

FAMOUS FIRSTS IN EARLY AVIATION

The first air-mail service was established by the U. S. Post Office between New York and Washington, D. C. on May 15, 1918. Major Reuben Fleet piloted the first flight and Lieutenant George Boyle made the return flight.

* * *

The first nonstop transatlantic flight was made by Captain John Alcock and Lieutenant Arthur Whitten Brown of England in a Vickers-Vimy biplane on June 14, 1919. They flew from Newfoundland to Clifden, Ireland, in 16 hours and 12 minutes.

* * *

The first nonstop transcontinental flight from New York to San Diego was made by Lieutenants Oakley Kelly and John Macready in May, 1923. Their trip in a Fokker T-2 took 26 hours and 50 minutes.

* * *

The first airplane flight over the North Pole was made on May 9, 1926. Lieutenant Floyd Bennett piloted a trimotor Fokker, commanded by Commander Richard E. Byrd, from Spitzbergen, Norway. During the 15 hours, before the plane returned to its base, it flew over the Pole.

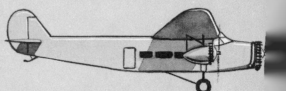

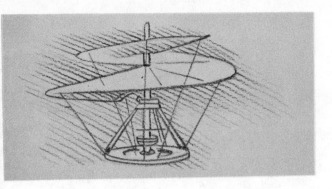

Da Vinci designed a helixpteron, the first helicopter.

The Launoy, or Chinese flying top, was the first successful model of a heavier-than-air machine that man built. It was the basis for the development of copters.

Flying in Any Direction

A helicopter can fly in any direction — straight up, straight down, forward, backward, sideways — and it can even stand still in mid-air. Furthermore, the helicopter can creep along a few inches above the ground or water, or it can climb thousands of feet into the sky and travel at over 100 miles per hour.

The fifteenth century genius, Leonardo da Vinci, not only designed a workable parachute and the ornithopter, but he also designed a very special flying machine. Overhead, it had a large screw-shaped propeller, which da Vinci hoped would screw into the air and lift the machine. He called this flying machine the *helixpteron* (hel-i-TER-on), which comes from the Greek *helix* (meaning "spiral") and *pteron* (meaning "wing").

How did the helicopter originate?

For more than two hundred fifty years no one paid attention to this idea. But in 1783, the French naturalist Launoy "discovered" a Chinese flying top, a toy probably brought back from the Orient. The top was made of feathers, wood and string and it could fly straight up. It was the first man-made heavier-than-air object that could leave the ground on its own power.

This top inspired George Cayley and he built a similar one, but used tin for the blades instead of feathers. The Cayley top rose 90 feet into the air.

All you need in order to make a Cayley top is a 6-inch model airplane propeller, an empty spool, a dowel that just about slides through the hole in the spool and a piece of string about 2 feet long.

How can you make a Cayley top?

Nail the propeller to one end of the dowel. Wind the string around the

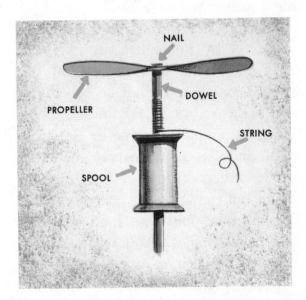

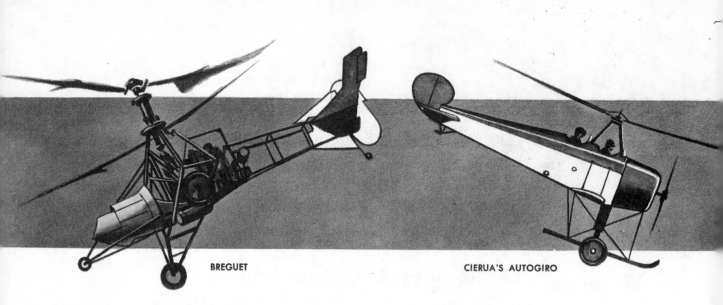

BREGUET   CIERUA'S AUTOGIRO

dowel, about an inch below the propeller. Then, slide the dowel into the spool. Hold the spool in one hand with the propeller pointing straight up. Pull the string hard and quickly with the other hand. The propeller spins and lifts the dowel straight into the air.

In 1878, Enrico Forlanini, using a pow-

Who were the early helicopter builders?

erful, tiny steam engine he designed and built, made a model helicopter. This steam-driven model hovered in the air at about 40 feet for 20 seconds. It provided positive proof that such a flying machine was possible.

The first full-sized helicopter to fly was built by Louis Breguet in 1907. This plane rose some 5 feet off the ground, but it could not be controlled and was unstable. It was not until 1922 that Russian-born George de Bothezat built and flew a helicopter that was stable and controllable. His *Flying Octopus,* built as a military helicopter, was an enormous ship with four rotors or horizontal blades. Although it made over one hundred successful flights from McCook Field in the United States, it

was abandoned because it was too clumsy and complicated.

The *autogyro* (auto-GY-ro) is a hybrid,

How does an autogyro fly?

a combination of an airplane and helicopter. Its Spanish inventor, Juan de la Cierva, used a small biplane and attached a set of whirling blades on top of the plane. There was no engine to work the top blades. They turned as the air from the propeller rushed passed them.

The turning of the rotary blades gave the plane extra lift or upward pull. For this reason, it was possible for the plane to take off at a slower engine speed and get into the air in less time. It appeared to jump into the air at take-off.

The autogyro's whirling blades turned only when the plane's propeller was spinning and, therefore, it hovered in the air. The only advantage of the autogyro was its ability to get into the air quickly at a lower engine speed. Although the autogyro has disappeared from the sky, the development of flexible rotary blades by Juan de la Cierva helped make it possible to build truly successful helicopters.

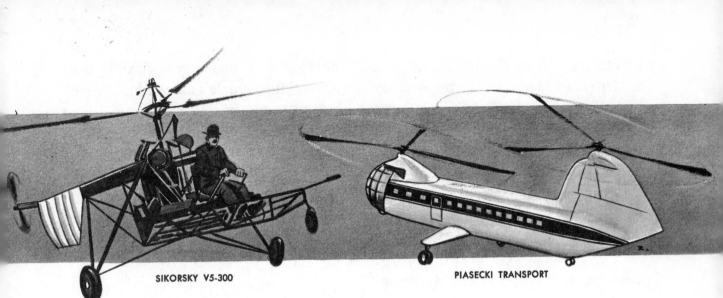

SIKORSKY V5-300

PIASECKI TRANSPORT

One man stands out in the history of helicopters — Igor Sikorsky. As a young man in Kiev, Russia, he built a model helicopter in 1910.

Who perfected the helicopter?

He continued to study the experiments of others and in 1939, working in the United States, he decided to try again.

For months, he worked on "Igor's Nightmare," as many people called his helicopter. He conducted many experiments and in May, 1940, he tried his first free flight. It was an overwhelming success compared with anything that preceded it. His ship could fly up, down, backward, sideways, and could hover in the air. But his ship had difficulty in flying forward. Additional work solved this problem and he started to produce workable helicopters.

World War II spurred the development of helicopters and in 1943, eighteen-year-old Stanley Hiller, Jr. designed and built the first coaxial helicopter. He used one engine to turn both rotors.

The helicopter is used to spray chemicals over crops to protect them from insects, to fight forest fires, to carry mail, to inspect power lines and pipe lines in rugged mountain country. It is also used in land- and sea-rescue work, by cowboys on very large ranches, and even acts as a "bus" between airports.

The rotor blades over the helicopter lift the ship and make it fly. The blades act somewhat like the wings of an airplane. The pilot of a helicopter can tilt these blades — this tilt is called *pitch*. Tilting the moving blades creates lift. If you have ever flown a kite, you know how this works.

How does the helicopter fly?

To climb into the air, the pilot tilts the moving blades and the helicopter goes straight up. When he wants to come down, he decreases the tilt, or pitch, of the blades. This decreases the lift, and gravity brings the ship down. If he wants to hover or stand still in the air, he sets the pitch of the blades so that the upward lift equals the pull toward the ground. Now, picture these moving blades as a saucer. You can tilt the entire saucer in any direction. It is through this tilting that the pilot can make the plane go forward, backward or sideways.

Near the tail of the helicopter is a smaller set of blades which revolve. By controlling their pitch, the pilot can keep the ship straight or make right and left turns.

A miniature helicopter is capable of

How do the modern ornithopters fly?

carrying one man. He can fly straight up, sideways, forward, backward, downward, or hover in the air. The personal *whirlywings* have been used experimentally by the U. S. Army for its scouts.

The *aerocycle,* another version of a one-man helicopter used by the Army, is somewhat larger than a *whirlywing* and the man stands on top of the cycle to fly it through the air.

This is a U. S. Army craft — a whirlywing.

Another small, one-man flying machine is the *flying platform*. It is shaped like a large doughnut and has a fan in the center. This fan lifts and propels the platform on which the man stands. The pilot's "leaning" controls the horizontal flight of this craft.

Air Cushion Vehicles (ACV's) are related-type hovering craft which move about suspended above a surface on a "cushion" of air. This cushion is formed by blowing a large volume of air down beneath the vehicle, using a fan, and

FLYING PLATFORM

holding it in place by a flexible skirt around the vehicle's outer edge. Propellers mounted in the ACV propel it at high speed.

Picture an airplane, higher than a three-story building, standing on

What is VTOL?

its tail. The propeller starts turning and soon the plane goes straight up into the air. Once the

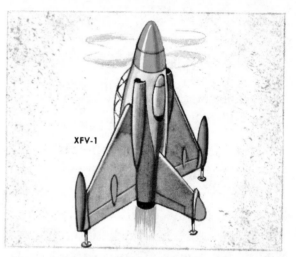

XFV-1

pilot gets up as high as he wants to go, he maneuvers the plane to a horizontal position and it flies like any ordinary airplane. Such planes, often called "flying pogo sticks," are VTOL aircraft. VTOL means "vertical take-off and landing." They can take off from land or any surface.

Not only can these planes take off and land vertically, but they can hover in the air as well. Also, they fly at speeds up to 500 miles per hour. Some VTOL aircraft are powered by rotors which tilt upward for takeoff and landing and tilt forward for horizontal flight. Some others have fans built into the wings which force air downward for vertical liftoff. Propellers or jet engines propel these aircraft forward.

Theory and Facts of Flight

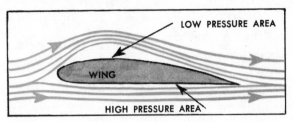

As the air rushes past the wing, or airfoil, it flows above and below the airfoil. The shape of the airfoil causes the air to travel a greater distance over the top of the foil. This results in a lowering of air pressure, which creates an upward lift on the airfoil.

Why does an airplane fly?

About forty years before the American Revolution, a Swiss scientist, Daniel Bernoulli, discovered that in any moving fluid the pressure is lowest where the speed is greatest. If we can increase the speed of air above a surface, such as a wing, pressure should decrease. The wing should rise.

In actual practice, the wing of an airplane is shaped somewhat like a bow — the upper surface is curved while the lower part is straight. Since the air has to travel a greater distance over the top part of the wing, it must travel at a greater speed. As a result, the pressure is lower above the wing than below it and the wing rises, or *lifts*, into the air. Engineers are constantly improving the shape of airplane wings for greater lift.

When an airplane flies horizontally, its propulsion system — a propeller or jet engine — must do two things. It must overcome the friction of the air in order to pull the plane forward, and it must move the plane fast enough forward to increase the speed of the air over the wings to create lift. Lift is the upward pressure on the wing. Lift overcomes *gravity* — the downward pressure created by the weight of the plane.

A propeller slices through the air in the same way that a screw cuts into wood, and pulls the plane forward. This forward motion of the propeller is called *thrust*. It counteracts the *drag* of the atmosphere, the force that resists forward motion.

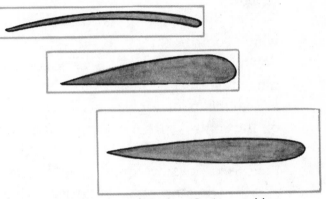

Airfoil cross sections, top to bottom: Design used by Wright brothers; "high-light" wing used on small planes; "high-speed" wing used by commercial liners. Improved wing designs result in higher speeds and smoother flights.

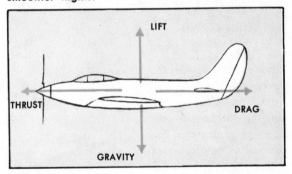

These four forces act upon a plane while in flight.

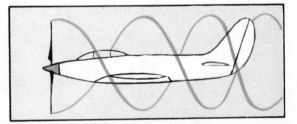

The propeller, called airscrews in England, provides the forward pulling or lifting power of an airplane.

An airplane, like any moving object following the basic laws of physics, tends to continue in a straight line unless some force is exerted to change its direction. The speed at which the engine turns the propeller is governed by the *throttle*. Opening the throttle increases the air speed and lifts the plane higher.

What makes an airplane go up and down?

Equally important is the *elevator* which controls the plane's upward and downward movement. It is a horizontal, hinged surface attached to the tail. When the pilot applies back pressure on the control stick, or column, the elevator is tilted upward. The air, striking the raised elevator, forces the tail down and the wing upward. The thrust of the propeller pulls the plane upward. Conversely, when the pilot pushes the control stick forward, the elevator is tilted downward. This forces the tail up and the wing down.

Two parts of an airplane control its turns to the right and left. The *rudder*, a vertical surface that is hinged to the tail, swings the tail to the right or left just in the same way as a section of the tail swings up or down. On the ground, it is used to make the plane turn just as a rudder of a boat does. In the air, however, the major purpose of the rudder is *not* to make the plane turn, but to assist the plane in entering and recovering from a turn.

How does an airplane turn?

The *ailerons,* small sections of the rear edge of the wing, near the tips, are hinged and are so connected that as one rises, the other lowers. This action tends to raise one wing and lower the other.

When the aileron on the right wing is lowered, the right wing rises and the plane will be tilted, or *banked,* to the left. The lifting force on the right wing is no longer completely upward — part of the force is pulling the plane to the left. This, in combination with the rudder, produces a left turn; that is, the plane is "lifted" around the turn.

The propeller provides the power for the forward thrust. The elevators enable the pilot to make the plane go up or down. The flaps aid in the ascent and help provide a smoother descent. The ailerons and rudder help the plane to turn left and right.

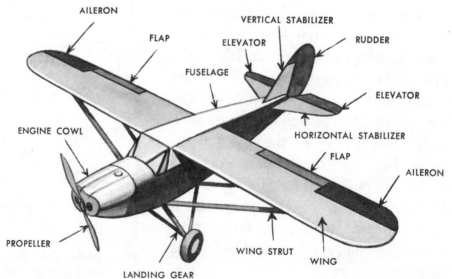

AILERON

FLAP

VERTICAL STABILIZER

ELEVATOR

RUDDER

FUSELAGE

ELEVATOR

ENGINE COWL

HORIZONTAL STABILIZER

FLAP

AILERON

PROPELLER

WING STRUT

WING

LANDING GEAR

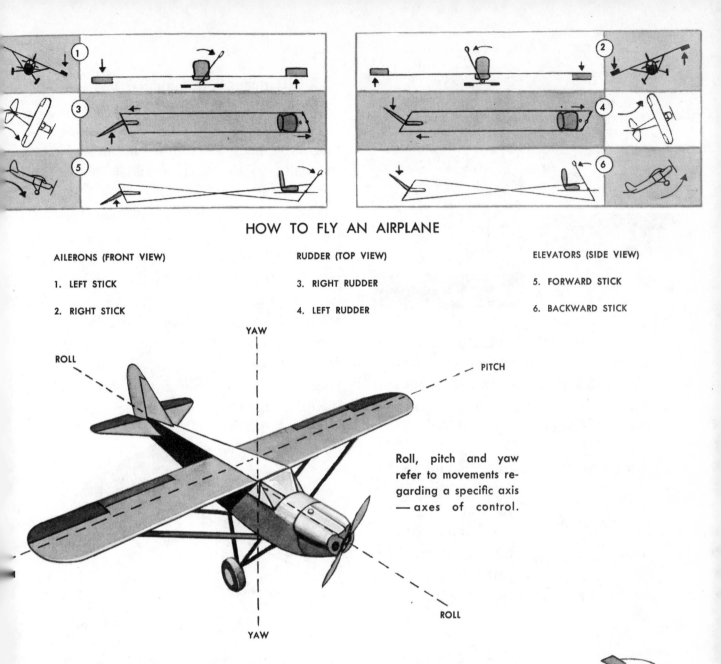

HOW TO FLY AN AIRPLANE

AILERONS (FRONT VIEW)	RUDDER (TOP VIEW)	ELEVATORS (SIDE VIEW)
1. LEFT STICK	3. RIGHT RUDDER	5. FORWARD STICK
2. RIGHT STICK	4. LEFT RUDDER	6. BACKWARD STICK

Roll, pitch and yaw refer to movements regarding a specific axis — axes of control.

How can you demonstrate lift? Take a piece of paper about 2 inches wide and about 5 inches long. Fold it an inch from the end. Hold the paper with your forefinger and thumb so that the fold is about an inch or two from your mouth. Blow with all your might over the top of the paper.

What happened? The paper moves up or *lifts*. By increasing the speed of the air over the top of the paper, you have reduced the pressure, causing the paper to rise.

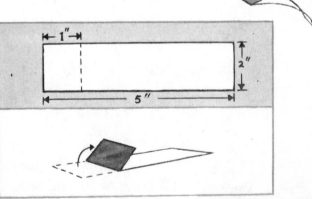

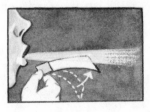

You can demonstrate lift, caused by the Bernoulli effect, on the upper surface of a piece of paper (right).

27

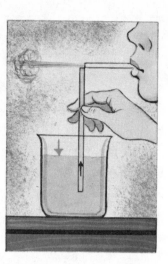

You can demonstrate this same principle with a simple atomizer. Blowing across the top of the tube — you can use a straw — reduces the pressure and causes the liquid to rise within the tube.

How can you demonstrate the working of an elevator?

Take a 3 by 5 index card and fold a 1-inch section along the long edge upward at a 45-degree angle. Paste the card, along its short center line, to a piece of balsa wood about 10 inches long. Balance the wood with the attached card on a round pencil, like a seesaw. Mark this "balance" point and push a straight pin through the balsa so that it is parallel to the card.

Hold the pin lightly between the thumb and forefinger of both hands. Hold the balsa wood in front of your mouth with the card farthest away. Now when you blow with all your might, the raised portion of the index card acts like a plane's elevator. The front end of the balsa wood (nearest your mouth) will move upward, like the nose of a plane.

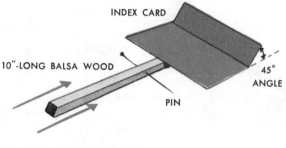

INDEX CARD
10"-LONG BALSA WOOD
PIN
45° ANGLE
DIRECTION FROM WHICH YOU BLOW

WHAT DO THE INSTRUMENTS TELL THE PILOT?

Here are only a few of the more important instruments which a pilot uses to guide his airplane:

Oil Pressure Gauge indicates the pressure of the oil in the engine. The dial is colored so that it is easier for the pilot to instantly spot any danger.

Oil Temperature Gauge tells the temperature of the oil in the engine.

Rate-of-Climb Indicator tells the pilot the speed at which his plane is climbing or dropping. The indicator is at zero when the plane is flying level.

Air Speed Indicator notes how fast the plane is moving through the air. Four colors are used for greater safety. Red is used to show maximum speed at which the plane can fly. Yellow shows a caution range — speeds approaching maximum speed. Heavy blue is used for normal cruising speeds. Light blue is used to show landing speed.

Turn-and-Bank Indicator is actually two separate instruments. The curved glass tube with a metal ball in liquid, the bank indicator, located near the bottom of the instrument, shows whether the plane is tilted to the right or left. The turn indicator shows the direction in which the nose of the plane is headed — to the left, straight ahead or to the right.

Instrument Landing System Indicator helps the pilot land his plane when the airfield is covered by fog or very low clouds. When the two pointers line up with the white circles on the dial, the plane is directly on path approaching the runway for a perfect landing.

Fuel Gauge indicates how much gasoline the plane has in its tank.

Tachometer tells the pilot how his motor is doing. It indicates the number of revolutions of the engine or the speed at which the propellers are turning.

Altimeter shows the height of the plane above the ground. There are three pointers — the smallest shows height in tens of thousands of feet above the ground; the medium-sized pointer shows height in thousands of feet; and the longest pointer shows height in hundreds and parts of hundreds of feet. The altimeter pictured here shows an altitude, or height, of 14,750 feet.

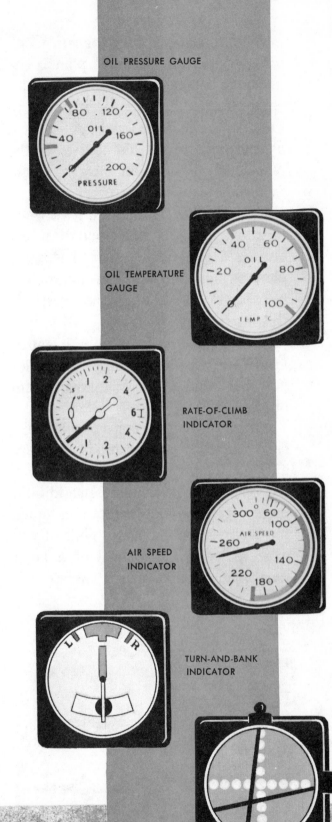

OIL PRESSURE GAUGE

OIL TEMPERATURE GAUGE

RATE-OF-CLIMB INDICATOR

AIR SPEED INDICATOR

TURN-AND-BANK INDICATOR

INSTRUMENT LANDING SYSTEM INDICATOR

ALTIMETER

TACHOMETER

FUEL GAUGE

Directional Gyro and Magnetic Compass are used to guide the plane. The magnetic compass acts like any regular compass you have seen — it points to the north. The directional gyro is used by the pilot to set his course. If the plane changes direction, the gyro shows this to the pilot.

Artificial Horizon helps a pilot when he is flying at night, in a cloud or in fog. During a clear day, a pilot keeps his plane straight and level by watching the horizon. At other times, he must use this instrument.

Drift Indicator is usually installed level with the floor. It shows the pilot how the wind might be blowing him off course.

In multi-engine, conventional aircraft, there is a separate oil pressure and oil temperature indicator and a tachometer for each engine. In addition, there is generally a separate fuel gauge for each tank in the plane. Thus, if you were to look at the panel of a large four-engine airliner which has six fuel tanks, you would see seventeen more instruments than you see here. Furthermore, there is an identical set of dials for the co-pilot in addition to the pilot, and on some planes a third set of dials is used for the navigator-engineer.

Highways of the Air

There are thousands of airports of many different kinds throughout the world. In the United States, the Federal Aviation Administration (FAA) classifies the airports according to the length of their runways. An airport with a runway of 1,500 to 2,300 feet is classified as a personal airport and is used only by small, light, private planes.

DIRECTIONAL GYRO AND
MAGNETIC COMPASS

ARTIFICIAL HORIZON

DRIFT INDICATOR

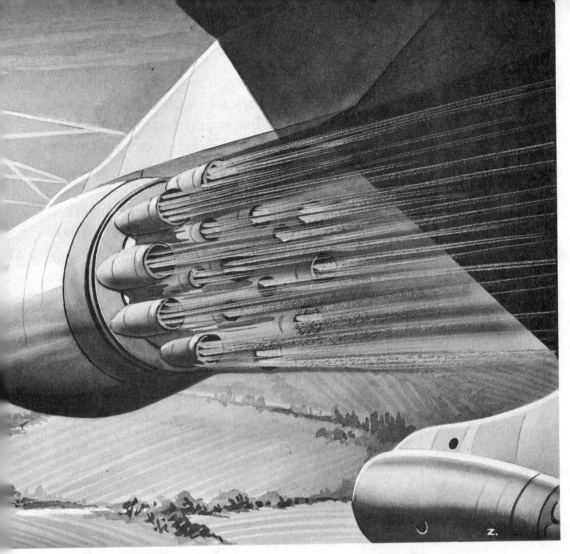

Airports range from the small grass fields for two- and four-passen-ger planes to the very large fields with concrete runways that handle the large commercial jet airliners.

Airports where large domestic passenger airliners can land and take off must have runways of 6,000 to 7,000 feet. To meet the needs of today's large jetliners, some airports have runways of 10,000 feet or more, or about two miles.

In the air between the airports are *airways,* or roads, **What are the airways?** through the sky along which the planes travel. Because of the many planes flying overhead, both during the day and night, it is necessary to set up rules for the road just as we have traffic rules for the cars on the streets.

Except when taking off or landing, airplanes must fly at least 500 feet above the ground. Over cities and other congested areas, the planes are required to fly 1,000 or even 2,000 feet above the ground.

The route a plane takes is determined by the FAA which controls all air traffic. At major airports, there are men sitting before air maps, radios and control boards, and they keep track of every plane as it plows through the skies.

Specific airways have been established to prevent planes from colliding in the air. All eastbound flights — planes flying from west to east — fly at *odd* thousand-foot levels, plus 500 feet, above sea level. Thus, a plane flying from Los Angeles to New York could fly at 15,500 feet. Westbound flights, on the other hand, fly at *even* thousand-foot levels, plus 500 feet, above sea level.

WHICH PLANE HAS THE RIGHT OF WAY?

Aircraft have rules that govern the right of way in the sky.

All flying craft have to give the right of way to a balloon.

Airplanes and airships have to give a glider the right of way.

An airplane must give an airship the right of way.

*   *   *

If two planes are flying so that their paths might cross, the plane to the right of the pilot has the right of way.

*   *   *

Should two planes be approaching head-on, both pilots must shift their planes to the right. As they pass, the planes must be at least 500 feet apart.

The same plane going from New York to Los Angeles could fly at 14,500 feet.

During a clear, sunny day — or Class C **How do air markers help pilots to fly?** weather according to the Air Weather Bureau — planes can fly by contact; that is, the pilot can see the ground and identify his route. There are various markers along the route on the ground. These markers also appear on special flight maps which the pilot carries with him just as we carry a road map in a car.

The air markers indicate location, have arrows pointing to the nearest air-

port and other identifying information. The markers are painted on highways, roofs of barns and factories, and the sides of high buildings such as grain elevators. They are also set in stone on mountains or in fields.

In addition to the visible markers, there is also radio contact. The CAA operates many radio stations throughout the country. By picking up different stations, the pilot can determine his exact position over the ground.

During the night, when it is clear, the pilot can spot visible ground markers, some of which are illuminated, special air beacons (similar to lights from a lighthouse) and airport lights and beacons.

Look into the cockpit of an airplane **How do pilots fly in all types of weather?** and you will see a maze of dials, knobs, switches and levers. These instruments and controls help the pilot at take-off, when he guides the plane safely through the airways and when he lands. Today's plane can land even when the pilot cannot see the airport.

The Instrument Landing System (ILS) is used when the airport's *ceiling* (the height from the ground to the clouds above) is too low for the pilot to land by sight. Through the use of electronic equipment, the pilot can "see" through the fog, rain, sleet and dark. A special instrument on his flight panel helps him align his airplane directly with the airport's runway. The instrument also shows him if he is too high or too low as he approaches.

Radar is also used to help pilots fly

through foul weather and to land safely. The major airports use Air Surveillance Radar (ASR) with which they can pinpoint the exact position in the sky of any plane within 60 miles of the airport. Some of the newer *blind landing* techniques (when the pilot cannot see the airport landing strip) involve automatic controls. The pilot sets the plane on special electronic instruments, and a ground controller, using radar, actually lands the plane.

Faster Than Sound

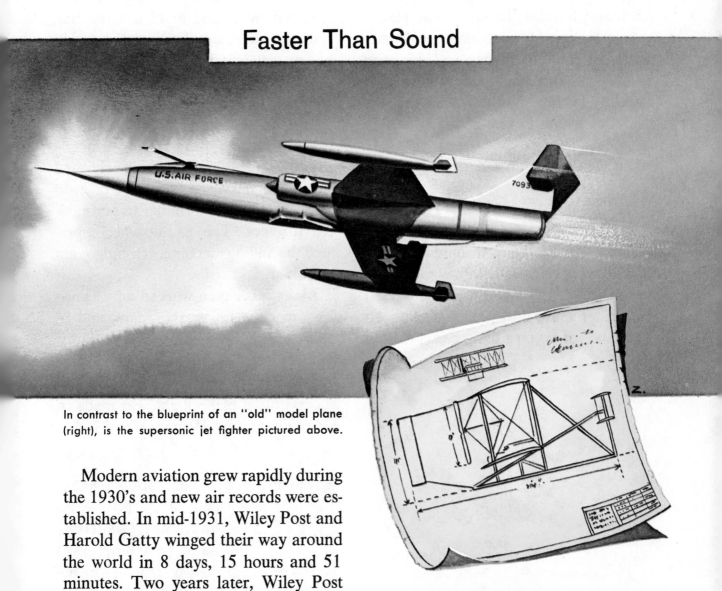

In contrast to the blueprint of an "old" model plane (right), is the supersonic jet fighter pictured above.

Modern aviation grew rapidly during the 1930's and new air records were established. In mid-1931, Wiley Post and Harold Gatty winged their way around the world in 8 days, 15 hours and 51 minutes. Two years later, Wiley Post set out by himself in his plane, the *Winnie Mae,* and made the same earthcircling trip in 7 days, 8 hours and 49 minutes. During this flight, he used two new aviation instruments — the radio compass and a robot or automatic pilot.

It has been said that the world was put on wings when the Douglas DC-3 was introduced in 1936. Until that time, the airlines used small planes, such as the Fokker trimotor and Ford trimotor. Each carried only eight people and

33

reached top speeds of about 100 miles an hour. The DC-3 carried twenty-one passengers in addition to a crew of three, and it could fly at 180 miles per hour. This "workhorse of the airlines" helped to build air passenger travel in the United States.

The outbreak of World War II in September, 1939 signaled a new era in aviation history. Emphasis was placed on faster fighter planes, on larger bombers that could fly higher, and on troop transports that could carry more men and fly farther. World War II saw the first jet planes in real action.

The idea of jet power, or propulsion, goes back to early history. The Greek mathematician, Hero, who lived in Alexandria about 130 B.C., is credited with being the first to build a jet engine. He converted steam pressure into jet action with an "engine" of his own design. It consisted

When were jets first used?

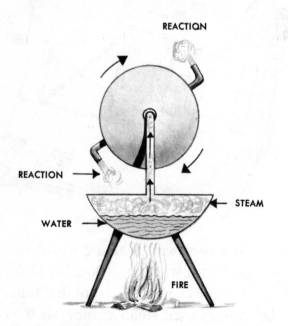

The "aeoliphile" was built by Hero of Alexandria.

of a hollow metal sphere which was mounted so that it could spin freely. The steam inside the sphere escaped through small nozzles, causing the sphere to spin. This engine was a scientific toy and was never put to use.

The jet principle was put to work during the Middle Ages in Europe. The *smoke-jack,* which some claim da Vinci invented, was used to turn a roasting spit in a fireplace. The turning action of the spit was produced by a fan in the chimney. The hot air passing up the chimney turned the fan.

In 1629, Giovanni Branca perfected a steam turbine using the jet principle to operate a milling machine. He used steam, which passed through a pipe, to turn a paddle-wheel similar to our modern turbines. The paddle-wheel operated the milling machine, crushing grain into flour.

Many other men worked on jet-powered machines over the years, and in 1926 an English scientist, Dr. Griffiths, proposed the use of jet-powered gas turbines to power an airplane. The first successful jet-plane flight was made in Germany when a Heinkel He-178 took to the air on August 27, 1939.

Have you ever pressed a spring together and let it go? What happens? It springs back to its original size. The air around us behaves in the same way. When you compress air, it tries to escape and expand to its original volume. When you heat air, it expands, and also tries to escape. Compressing and heating air give the jet engine its power.

How does a jet fly?

If you take an inflated balloon and let it go, the air inside the balloon will escape. As it rushes out, the balloon "flies" through the air. This illustrates the principle which makes the jet fly. It is an example of Newton's third law of motion: "For every action, there is an equal and opposite reaction." As the air rushes out the back, the balloon goes forward.

The balloon's activity is a form of jet propulsion.

There are several types of jet engines and all work on the same principle. A jet plane needs no propeller since it uses air to give it forward motion or thrust. The most common type of jet engine is the turbojet.

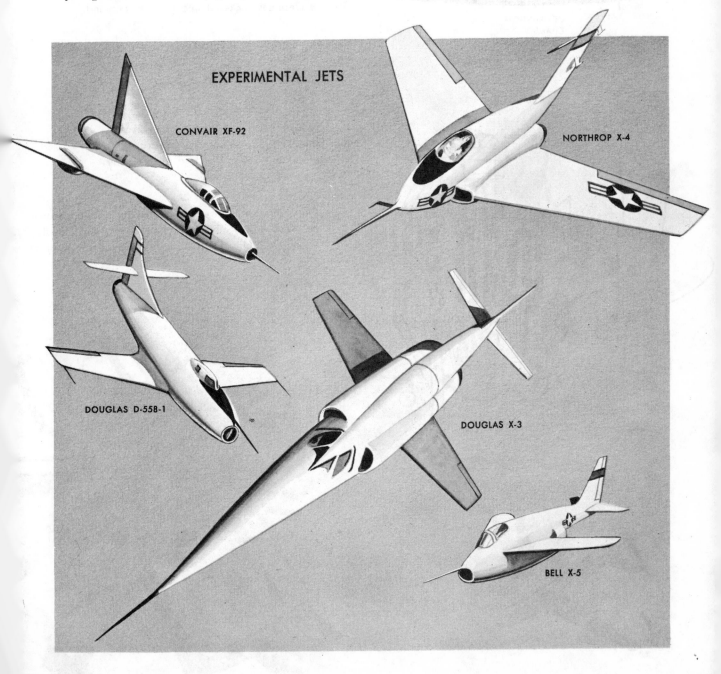

EXPERIMENTAL JETS

CONVAIR XF-92

NORTHROP X-4

DOUGLAS D-558-1

DOUGLAS X-3

BELL X-5

RAMJET AND PULSEJET

The *ramjet* is the simplest of all jet engines. It has no moving parts. The air is compressed by the forward motion of the plane. The plane has to be in motion *before* the ramjet works. Therefore, a plane with a ramjet engine has to be launched in the air by a "mother ship."

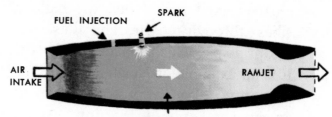

The *pulsejet* is also a simple jet engine. It has only one moving part, an inlet valve which controls the amount of air entering the engine. It was first used during World War II to power the V-1 flying bombs which the Germans rocketed into London, England.

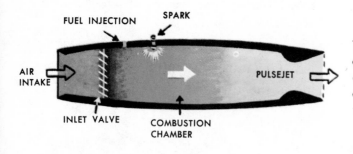

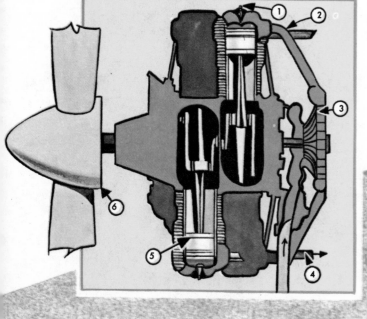

A reciprocating engine: (1) spark plug; (2) cylinder inlet; (3) shaft-driven supercharger; (4) cylinder exhaust; (5) piston; and (6) propeller.

Super aircraft require special aircraft facilities. Shown below is a typically modern structure which handles traffic at John F. Kennedy International Airport.

Modern jet planes, like the Douglas DC-8, are rapidly changing aviation history. With modern jet passenger planes, it is possible to carry more people greater distances in less time.

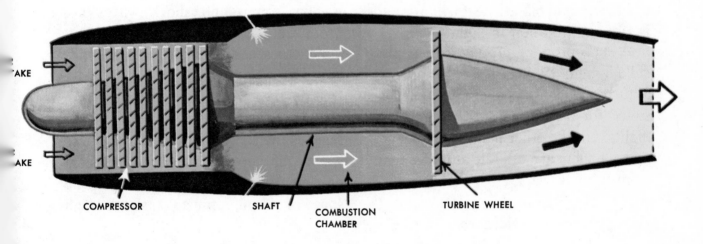

AKE

AKE

COMPRESSOR   SHAFT   COMBUSTION CHAMBER   TURBINE WHEEL

HOW A TURBOJET WORKS

1. Air is sucked into the engine through the front intake. The compressor, acting like a large fan, compresses the air and forces it through ducts, or tubes, to the combustion chamber.

2. In the combustion chamber, fuel is sprayed into the compressed air and ignited. The resulting hot gases expand rapidly and, with terrific force, blast their way out of the rear of the engine. This jet blast gives the engine and plane its forward thrust.

3. As the hot gases rush out of the engine, they pass through a set of blades, the turbine wheel. These blades react like a windmill and turn the main engine shaft, which operates the front compressor.

4. Some engines, designed to give extra pushing power, have an afterburner attached to the engine. This is a long tail cone in which more fuel is sprayed and burned, just before the gases pass through the rear exhaust.

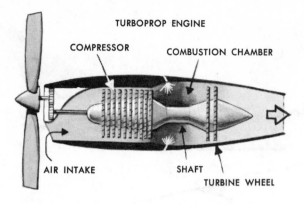

TURBOPROP ENGINE
COMPRESSOR COMBUSTION CHAMBER
AIR INTAKE SHAFT TURBINE WHEEL

A *turboprop* is a jet engine connected to a conventional propeller. It combines the advantages of a gas turbine jet with those of a propeller. During take-off and low speeds, the propeller produces higher forward thrust. During landing, the propeller creates greater drag, enabling the plane to take off and land in shorter distances than a turbojet. However, the gas turbine jet is lightweight as compared with a conventional plane's piston motor and is without vibration in flight.

Why do they use turboprops?

A turboprop, or *propjet* as it is also called, cannot fly as fast or as high as a turbojet. Turbojets are particularly suited for high-speed and high-altitude flights. On the other hand, propjets are more efficient at moderate altitudes than conventional piston-engine planes.

Have you ever noticed that during a lightning storm you can see the flash of lightning before you hear the thunder? This is because light travels faster than sound. The speed of sound in freezing air (32°F.) is about 1,090 feet per second or 743 miles per hour. The speed of sound increases as the temperature rises, about a foot a second faster for each degree. At 68°F.,

What is the sound barrier?

the speed of sound in air is about 1,130 feet per second or 765 miles per hour.

Sound travels through the air in waves similar to those produced when you drop a stone into a pond. One of the people who studied sound and air waves was an Austrian professor of physics, Ernest Mach. About 1870, he photographed cannon shells flying through the air in order to discover what happens to an object as it speeds through the air. He found that the moving object produced *shock waves*. The object pushes against the molecules in the air. As one molecule is pushed, it in turn pushes the others near it. Imagine a long line of boys standing one behind the other. The last boy in the line gets pushed. As he moves forward, he pushes the boy in front of him. This happens all the way down the line. This is how sound and shock waves are produced.

As the speed of a plane approaches the speed of sound, it is pushing rapidly against the molecules in the air and creating shock waves. As the plane reaches the same speed as sound, these waves pile up and form an invisible barrier. When the plane exceeds the speed of sound, it must "crash" through

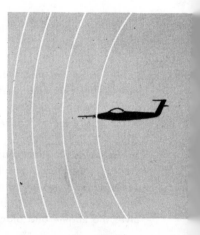

As the plane goes through the air, it creates sound waves. The plane itself displaces air about it as it speeds forward.

this barrier. As it does, it creates a thunderlike sound. You will see the plane before you hear its motor, just as you see lightning before you hear the thunder.

As planes began to fly higher and faster,

How did the sound barrier change the shape of planes?

the planes vibrated fiercely and the pilots had difficulty operating the controls. These pilots had encountered *wave drag*, the piling-up of air in front of the plane. Scientists and airmen studied this effect on planes and soon recognized what was happening.

To honor the man who first explored this subject scientifically, we measure the speed of a plane or rocket in *Mach numbers*. Aeronautical engineers use Mach 1 as equal to 680 miles per hour, the speed of sound at about 35,000 feet and higher, where the temperature is 50° or lower. Mach 2 equals twice the speed of sound or 1,360 miles per hour.

They found that the shock waves which caused wave drag were shaped like a cone. If the plane has long wings, it tends to spin more easily. As a result, jet planes, designed to fly faster than sound, have shorter wings set farther

back along the sides of the body. These wings sweep back from the sides of the airplane to conform to the shape of the shock wave. This increases the speed of the airplane and makes it more stable.

Scientists have studied sound waves and plane speeds in special wind tunnels using model planes, and thus, have helped engineers to develop better planes.

As planes climbed higher into the air,

Why do planes fly in the jet stream?

meteorologists (weather men) and pilots discovered fast-moving "rivers of air" between 25,000 and 40,000 feet above the earth. These rivers generally flow in an east-west direction and reach speeds of almost 300 miles per hour. Since the jet planes were the first to

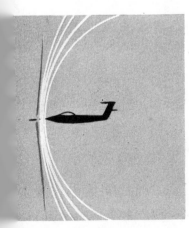

As the plane's speed is increased, approaching at the speed of sound, it is increasing the compression of the sound waves.

As the speed of the plane exceeds that of the waves it created, it then plunges headlong through the sound barrier.

reach such high altitudes, these "rivers" became known as the *jet stream*.

A plane flying in the same direction as the jet stream is carried along in much the same way as you are carried by a strong wind when you are walking with it on a very windy day. A plane flying 600 miles per hour with the jet stream traveling 300 miles per hour, is actually traveling 900 miles an hour over the earth. The jet stream helps conserve fuel and shorten flying time.

What will future jet planes be like? Revolutions in jet plane design are already taking place. One of the ships that North American Aviation is building is the B-70, half plane and half spaceship. This versatile craft, with a 156-foot pencil-thin body, is planned as a nuclear bomber with a range of 7,000 miles.

Another remarkable change is the development of an airbreathing aircraft wing. As the conventional aircraft wing slices through the air at supersonic speeds, the air around the wing becomes choppy or turbulent. This turbulence creates a drag on the wing, causing the plane to slow up. With the new wing design, there is a smooth flow of air over and under the wing. This smoother flight will require less fuel so that planes will be able to fly more economically.

What is an SST? An SST is a "supersonic transport," an airliner that can fly faster than the speed of sound. France and England, working together, built an SST which has flown successfully. At cruising speed the plane will be flying 1,800 miles per hour and it will be at an altitude of nearly twelve miles.

The SST needs very long runways: 1 mile to take off and 1¼ miles to land.

An SST can fly across the Atlantic Ocean in 2½ hours. The SST has not been accepted, however, because it is very expensive and people object to the noise caused by its *sonic boom*. Also, people do not like to fly that fast.

The wide-bodied "Jumbo Jets" are very fast and carry as many as three hundred people at one time. They have been very popular and are now used by most airlines. The largest is the Boeing 747. The Douglas DC-10 and the Lockheed L-1011 are also used by many airlines for long-distance flights.

RECENT AVIATION HISTORY

Between January 16 and 18, 1957, three U. S. Air Force B-52's, led by Major General Archie J. Old, Jr., flew nonstop around the world. They were refueled in flight by tanker airplanes which met them at several points on their route. The 24,325-mile flight took 45 hours and 19 minutes. The longest flight on a single fueling was made by Major Sidney J. Kubesch, who flew a B-52 from Tokyo over the Arctic to London, an 8,028-mile trip which took 8 hours and 35 minutes. The longest distance in a straight line, 12,532 miles, was flown by Major Clyde R. Evely, in a USAF B-52, from Kadena, Okinawa, to Madrid, Spain, on January 10 and 11, 1962.

* * *

Captain Joseph W. Kittinger, Jr., a thirty-one-year-old United States Air Force officer, soared nearly 103,000 feet above the New Mexico desert in an open-gondola balloon on August 16, 1960. He exceeded the old record set by Lieutenant Colonel David G. Simons, using a closed-gondola balloon, by some 500 feet.

After reaching the record height, Kittinger plunged toward the earth. He set a new world's record for free fall (jumping with a parachute closed). He plunged some 17 miles in 4 minutes and 38 seconds. Upon reaching about 17,500 feet, he opened his parachute and descended the remainder of his trip in 8 minutes and 30 seconds.

A new height-record for a balloon was set May 4, 1961 by Navy Commanders Malcolm Ross and Victor Prather. Their helium-filled balloon, with an aluminum-framed gondola, soared to 113,739 feet. Prather was killed during the helicopter rescue.

On March 5, 1962, Captain Robert G. Sowers flew a Convair B-58 *Hustler* from Los Angeles to New York in 2 hours and 59 minutes. Then, without stopping, he flew back to Los Angeles, making the round trip in 4 hours, 41 minutes, 15 seconds.

* * *

A world record for altitude in horizontal flight was set on May 1, 1965, by Air Force Colonel R. L. Stephens, who flew a Lockheed YF-12A at 80,257.86 feet.

* * *

The longest helicopter flight was made in a Hughes YOH6A, from Culver City, California, to Daytona, Florida, on April 6-7, 1966.

* * *

During the summer of 1966, an X-15 rocket aircraft soared to a height of 324,200 feet, more than 61 miles above the earth, setting a manned winged-craft record. On October 3, 1967, an X-15 flown by Major William J. Knight, USAF, attained a speed of 4,534 miles per hour at Edwards Air Force Base, California.

* * *

Since the days of Daedalus, man has sought to fly with his "own wings." So far, the nearest man has come to this dream has been the one-man helicopter. The Gyrodyne YRON-1 *Rotorcycle* is now in full production for both the United States Navy and the Marine Corps. This small helicopter carries one man easily and can carry heavy loads in addition. It is now being used for map plotting and military observation, and will be used for anti-submarine missions by the United States Navy.

KITTINGER BALLOON

BELL X-15

McDONNELL F4H-1

BOEING 707

DOUGLAS DC-8

GYRODYNE ROTORCYCLE

Rockets, Missiles and Satellites

How were rockets first used? Some historians believe that the Chinese used rockets, similar to our large firecrackers, at about the same time that the ancient Egyptians were building the Great Pyramids. They attached the rockets to arrows to make them fly farther. We do know that in A.D. 1232, during the Mongolian siege of the city of Kaifêng, the Chinese used *fei-i-ho-chien* (sticks of flying fire) to defend themselves. In fourteenth-century Europe, military rockets were used to set fire to cities and terrorize the enemy.

One of the most famous early uses of military rockets was at the Battle of Fort McHenry during the War of 1812. The British launched rockets from boats in conjunction with artillery fire. During the rocket attack, Francis Scott Key, writing the words to the "Star-Spangled Banner," described the red glare of the rockets. Some forty years later, military rockets began to disappear as weapons, because artillery cannons became more efficient.

The first man to attempt to fly a rocket ship was a Chinese mandarin, Wanhu. About A.D. 1500, he had a bamboo chair "rocket ship" to which forty-seven of the largest rockets available were attached. He sat in the chair and held a large kite in each hand. The kites were to help him glide gently back to earth. At a signal, his assistants ignited the rockets. It is reported that there was a great roar, a blast of flame and smoke — and Wanhu and his ship disappeared. It is unlikely that he flew into space.

Who were the rocket pioneers? Although rockets disappeared as military weapons shortly after the Mexican War in 1847, they continued to be used for signaling at sea during distress, as flares to light battlefields and as fireworks. But the dream of space continued.

An American physicist, Dr. Robert Goddard, began to experiment with rockets in 1908. In 1919, when he published his first report, he revolutionized rocket theory. Up to that time, scientists believed that a rocket flew because its explosion pushed against the air. Dr. Goddard noted that rockets could fly even in "thin" air similar to that found

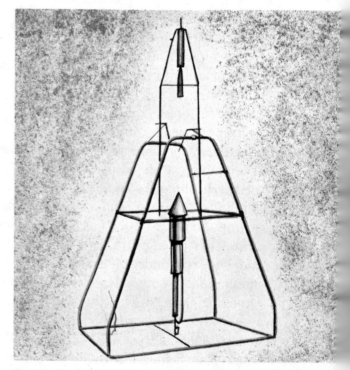

Goddard's first liquid fuel rocket was fired in 1926.

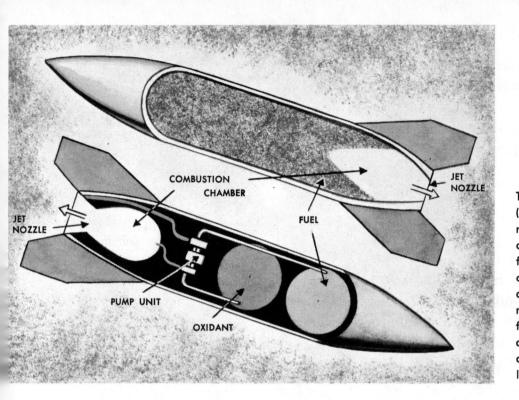

Labels on the diagram:
COMBUSTION CHAMBER
JET NOZZLE
JET NOZZLE
FUEL
PUMP UNIT
OXIDANT

The solid fuel rocket (top) is used for short-range guided missiles and as assisting devices for quick take-off of conventional and jet aircraft. The liquid fuel rocket (below) is used for long-range flights and when high speeds are needed, as in launching satellites.

thousands of feet above the earth. He believed that rockets could be flown to the moon.

Although people ridiculed him and his work, Dr. Goddard continued to experiment. In 1926, he tested the first liquid fuel rocket. It traveled at 60 miles per hour and reached 184 feet in the air. His report and work inspired others in the field of rocketry. In 1929, in Germany, a rocket-propelled glider carried a man in flight.

In 1935, Dr. Goddard launched a gyroscope-controlled rocket. It rose almost 8,000 feet and attained a speed of almost 700 miles per hour. About the same time, a group of Germans interested in rockets formed the *Verein für Raumschiffahrt,* the Rocket Society. One of its members was Dr. Wernher von Braun who, during World War II, directed rocket research at the German Research Facility at Peenemünde. After the war, von Braun came to the United States where he played a major role in its rocket and space programs.

The basic rocket engine contains a combustion chamber and an exhaust nozzle. It needs no moving parts.

What makes a rocket fly?

The burning of the propellant (explosive charge or fuel) escaping from the exhaust creates forward thrust.

Rockets are classified into two general groups — solid propellant and liquid propellant. The first group, solid propellants, are somewhat like the large firecrackers used on the Fourth of July. These rockets are powered by a rapidly burning powder or solid.

Liquid propellant rockets have more complex power units. It is necessary to have tanks within the rockets to hold the liquid and pumps and valves to control the flow of the liquid to the combustion chamber. The Saturn 1B and Saturn 5 launch vehicles, which are the workhorses of the U.S. space program, use liquid hydrogen for fuel. This is mixed with liquid oxygen (*LOX*) in flight to produce combustion and provide power for the rocket.

43

Because the rockets carry their own oxygen to aid combustion, they can work even in a vacuum, where there is no air. Only the amount of fuel limits the height they can reach.

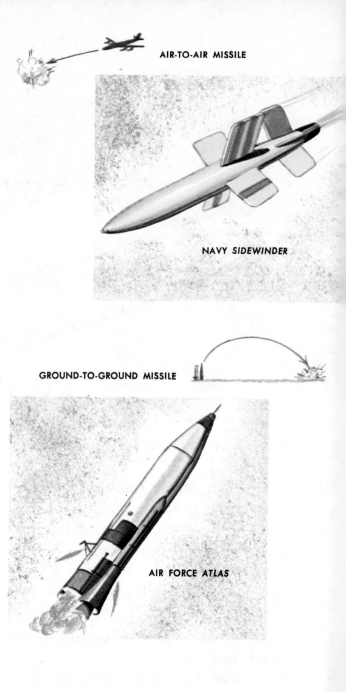

AIR-TO-AIR MISSILE

NAVY *SIDEWINDER*

GROUND-TO-GROUND MISSILE

AIR FORCE *ATLAS*

What is a guided missile? Any rocket whose flight path can be altered in flight is known as a *guided missile*. The Germans' V-1 rockets used during World War II were actually pulsejet engines with explosive warheads to bombard London. These missiles flew at 360 miles per hour and had a range of about 150 miles. The German V-2 rockets were larger and more powerful. Their range was about 200 miles and they reached speeds of 3,600 miles per hour. Once launched, they followed a predetermined ballistic trajectory.

One system of classifying guided missiles is based on (a) where they are fired, and (b) the location of their target. For example, *surface-to-surface* missiles are fired from the ground to hit a target on the ground. Examples of surface-to-surface missiles are the Air Force *Atlas* and *Titan*. Both have a range of 8,000 to 8,500 miles and travel at a speed of over Mach 20 — twenty times the speed of sound. The Navy's *Polaris* is a surface-to-surface missile that can be fired from under water.

Surface-to-air missiles include the Navy's *Talos* and the Army's *Hercules*, which travel at speeds of over Mach 3 and Mach 4. The Navy's *Sidewinder*, which exceeds a Mach 2.5 speed, is an *air-to-air* missile, while the Army's *Rascal* is an *air-to-surface* missile.

How do they guide missiles? Many guided missiles are controlled in flight by radio, radar, and electronic computers. When one radar beam picks up the target, it feeds the information about height, direction and speed to a computer. The electronic computer makes all the cal-

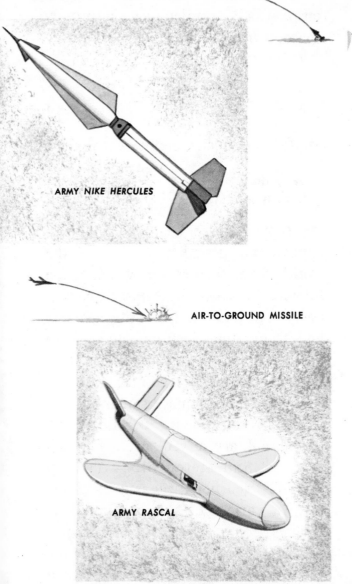

GROUND-TO-AIR MISSILE

ARMY *NIKE* HERCULES

AIR-TO-GROUND MISSILE

ARMY RASCAL

culations within seconds and fires the missile. The missile is "watched" in flight by another radar beam, which tells the computer the missile's flight. The computer makes changes in the missile's path by using radio waves which control adjustment motors within the missile.

A similar radar, radio and electronic computer system is used to launch and guide rockets as they go off into space. Large radar and radio telescope units "follow" the rocket as it plunges into space. If the rocket veers off course, these watchers inform the computer and it radios the rocket, making the necessary changes to correct its course.

Why does a satellite stay up in the sky? If you throw a ball into the air, the pull of gravity will bring it back to earth. Also, a moving body will continue to travel in a straight line unless acted on by another force. These two principles govern the orbiting of satellites.

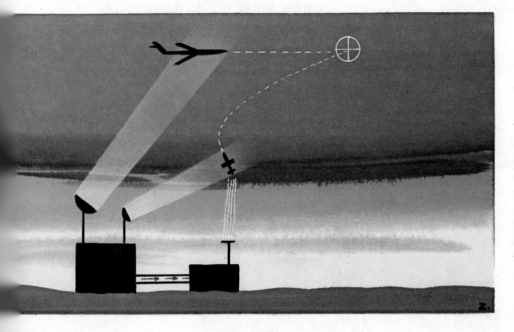

The main radar scanner (left) picks up approaching aircraft. A computer works out the plane's speed, path, height, weather conditions and other factors. The ground missile is automatically made ready and fired by the computer. A smaller radar guides the missile through the air until it reaches the enemy target.

If the ball were shot up like a rocket, it would be affected by these two forces. One is the force of gravity that would pull it back to earth, and the other is the force that would tend to keep it moving in a straight line. Suppose the ball traveled at a speed of 18,000 miles per hour at a height of 300 miles. At this speed and at this height, these two forces would be about equal, or balanced. As a result, the ball would continue to "orbit" the earth. That is what a satellite does.

The speed needed to completely overcome the earth's gravitational pull is called the *escape velocity*. This is the velocity that the body needs to attain to overcome the pull of gravity. That escape velocity from the earth is about 25,000 miles per hour. Thus, for a satellite to remain in orbit, it must attain a speed of at least 18,000 miles per hour. If it is to escape the earth's gravitational pull in order to go into outer space, it must be traveling at over 25,-000 miles per hour.

Man's first artificial satellite was *Sputnik 1*, launched October 4, 1957 by the Soviet Union. The event made large headlines in newspapers and periodicals all over the world. Since then, so many man-made satellites have been sent into space that computers are used to identify each one and keep count. Such launchings have become so commonplace today that most people hardly take note of them.

Why do we launch satellites?

In general, man-made satellites serve as aids for scientific investigation, navigation, military surveillance, communications, and meteorology (which includes weather forecasting). They have a variety of shapes, including spheres, cones, cylinders, and spheres with paddles. *Echo 1*, launched by the United States in August, 1960, was a giant balloon which was put into orbit to aid long-range voice communications by bouncing radio-wave telephone messages off its massive surface.

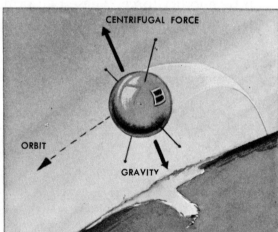

Rockets carry satellite into the air so it can take off under its own power. The satellite is kept in orbit as the centrifugal force is balanced by the gravitational pull of the earth.

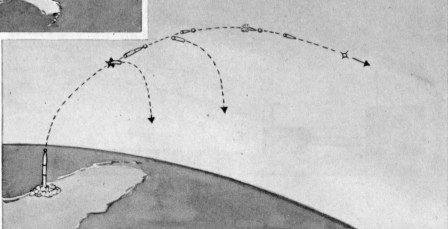

Satellites all carry some kind of radio transmitter which emits signals. Such signals can pinpoint a satellite's exact position in space or relay information gathered by instrumentation. Many satellites can also receive signals which will activate (or deactivate) instruments by remote control.

The accomplishments of satellites have been many and varied. They have discovered hurricanes and tracked them, so that communities in the path of such storms could be forewarned and take steps to protect lives and property. They have discovered and mapped the Van Allen belt of radiation in space. They have measured temperature, water vapor content, and ozone in the earth's atmosphere. They have made possible "live" television across vast oceans. They are mapping the earth, the moon, and the planets in new ways and are even reaching back in time to observe the fiery birth of the universe.

Steppingstones Into Space

On October 14, 1947, six miles up in the sky over California, a four-engine B-29 airplane was flying its prescribed course. Fastened to its underside was a smaller plane, painted bright orange. Suddenly, the orange plane, powered by a rocket engine using liquid oxygen and alcohol as fuel, soared upward like a stone fired from a slingshot. That plane was the Bell X-1, a rocket ship piloted by U.S. Air Force Captain Charles E. Yeager. Space and aviation history was made that day as the craft exceeded Mach 1, the speed of sound.

When did man first fly faster than sound?

Six years later, Lt. Colonel Marion Carl flew a Douglas *Skyrocket* to an altitude of 83,235 feet (in August), and made the first flight at *twice* the speed of sound in the same supersonic aircraft (in November).

Other rocket ships included the X-3, the *Flying Stiletto,* and the X-5, the *Flying Guppy.*

In 1963, the X-15, an outstanding rocket ship, was flown to an unofficial height of 354,200 feet by test pilot Joseph A. Walker.

On April 12, 1961, the Soviet Union launched *Vostok 1,* a five-ton space vehicle carrying Yuri A. Gagarin into an orbit around the earth. This spurred the United States into establishing its own space program. The program's goal was ambitious, but carefully planned — to land a man on the moon within the decade and return him safely to earth. Three separate projects, each taking advantage of the knowledge gained from the previous project, were set up by the National Aeronautics and Space Administration (NASA). Each consisted of a series of space flights that would test the endurance, adaptability and skill of the astronauts — the men assigned to make the trip — as well as

What were the first manned space flights?

establish space flight procedures and techniques, and solve technical problems. The names given to these projects were: *Project Mercury, Project Gemini,* and *Project Apollo.*

The *Mercury* passenger compartment (which came to be called the capsule) carried but one person. Navy Commander Alan B. Shepard, Jr., riding the vehicle named *Freedom 7,* launched by a modified Redstone rocket, became the first American astronaut. His flight was suborbital — it did not make a complete revolution around the earth — but where the *Vostok 1* orbital flight had been ground-controlled, this one was controlled by the pilot.

A 22-revolution flight by Gordon Cooper on May 15, 1963 completed the series of flights under *Project Mercury.*

Project Gemini teamed two men in orbital flight. Notable achievements included a "walk in space" by Edward White, and a rendezvous in space by *Gemini 6* and *Gemini 7* that successfully joined ("docked") the two spacecraft. The *Gemini 7* flight lasted two weeks.

Three-man space flights finally became a reality with *Project Apollo,* making it possible for man to attain his long-cherished dream of landing on the moon and exploring it.

The lunar module was the vehicle actually used to land **How did men land on the moon?** astronauts on the moon's surface and take them away from it. A Saturn 5 launch vehicle was used to escape the earth's gravity and place an *Apollo* spacecraft directly into lunar orbit. Astronauts then detached the lunar module and descended safely to the moon's surface. This same vehicle was later launched to a return rendezvous with the orbiting mother ship, which then used a rocket engine to escape the moon's gravity pull and return to Earth.

By this means did Neil Armstrong and Edwin E. ("Buzz") Aldrin, first men to walk the moon, effect their landing in the lunar module named *Eagle,* July 20, 1969.

Six more flights were made to the moon after the successful flight of *Apollo 11.* Only one, *Apollo 13,* did not land on the moon. Trouble developed in the spacecraft when it was 205,000 miles from earth, and it returned safely to earth without making the moon landing. During the remaining trips to the moon, astronauts performed scientific experiments, measured winds, temperature, and other conditions on the lunar surface, and returned with rocks found there for study by scientists.

To help men travel around on the moon's surface more easily, engineers at NASA's Marshall Space Flight Center, Huntsville, Alabama, designed a collapsible vehicle which was mounted on the lunar lander. When they arrived on the moon, the astronauts lowered the vehicle onto the surface. It looked very much like a dune buggy. They used it to travel greater distances on the moon than they could walk and to explore more of the moon's surface.

THE HOW AND WHY WONDER BOOK OF

ROCKETS AND MISSILES

by Clayton Knight

with additional text by
JOHN C. GOODRUM

Additional pictures by
U.S. ARMY, U.S. NAVY,
U.S. AIR FORCE, NASA

GROSSET & DUNLAP
Publishers • NEW YORK

INTRODUCTION

This book is one in a series of *How and Why Wonder Books* for young readers dealing with subjects of current interest in science and technology. Through authentic text and illustrations, it presents brief answers to several dozen important questions about rockets and missiles.

It reminds us that man's knowledge about the universe is vast. Yet new and exciting developments are announced every day, evidence that science is moving ahead at a remarkable pace. We know that there is still much more to be learned. Scientists throughout the world are seeking relentlessly for a new and better understanding about things in nature, ranging in their search from the tiniest atom to the limits of outer space. And as the answers to "how" and "why" questions are found, they provide further interesting knowledge that is useful for controlling our environment.

Children also ask "How?" and "Why?" They are curious to learn more and more about the world. And parents — to satisfy their own interest and to stimulate and keep up with youth — must be informed about modern advances of science as well. Fortunately, through books, parents and children can read and study together.

Learning the *how's* and *why's* in one field of scientific exploration usually leads to interest in other fields. This is to the good because it is important for young people in making career choices to know about the many opportunities in science. This book on rockets and missiles is one which will open new horizons for every reader and encourage further reading and exploration in related fields.

Paul E. Blackwood

Dr. Blackwood is a professional employee in the U. S. Office of Education. This book was edited by him in his private capacity and no official support or endorsement by the Office of Education is intended or should be inferred.

Library of Congress Catalog Card No.: 71-124649

ISBN: 0-448-05005-6 (Wonder Edition)
ISBN: 0-448-04004-2 (Trade Edition)
ISBN: 0-448-03825-8 (Library Edition)
1983 PRINTING

HOW OLD IS THE ROCKET PRINCIPLE?

HISTORICAL records show that as early as 800 years before Christ, the Chinese — who were the first to discover gunpowder — were shooting powder-packed tubes on a stick into the air to amuse their people.

These rockets followed all three of Sir Isaac Newton's three laws of motion. Mainly, however, it was Newton's third law which was in effect: For every *action*, there is an equal and opposite *reaction*. Thus, when the rocket's burning gases thrust *downward*, the opposite reaction is a thrust *upward*, sending the rocket in a fiery arc into the night sky.

In the 1700's William Congreve, in England, tested improved Chinese rockets as weapons of war. They achieved little success at the time, although when Francis Scott Key wrote the *Star Spangled Banner* during the War of 1812, the phrase, "the rockets' red glare" referred to Congreve missiles fired by the British against Fort McHenry.

The real father of modern rocketry was the American, Dr. Robert Goddard, a physics professor who, in the early 1900's, began experiments with rockets to send weather-recording instruments higher than meteorological balloons had ever gone.

He tried both solid fuel (powder) and liquid fuel (gasoline and oxygen), and in 1926 the world's first liquid-propelled rocket was successfully fired at Auburn, Massachusetts.

Starting with his first crude apparatus, he went on to add guidance features, an automatic parachute to bring recording instruments back to earth safely, and subsequently developed the principle of the multi-stage rocket which was eventually the means used to launch spacecraft and men on exciting journeys to the moon.

Goddard's first rocket

WHAT ARE THE DIFFERENT KINDS
OF ROCKET FUELS?

THE only engine capable of operating in airless space is the rocket which needs no outside air for combustion. In place of atmosphere, the rocket must have an oxidizer to make the fuel burn — usually liquid oxygen, which must be kept at 272 degrees below zero, F., and must be handled carefully.

Rockets burning solid fuels demand less care, but the fuel combustion is more difficult to control.

The first rocket engines had moderate thrust, delivering about six thousand pounds. The *Apollo* astronauts flying to the moon began their space journey on a *Saturn 5* rocket thrusting seven and a half *million* pounds! Nuclear rockets will be even more powerful.

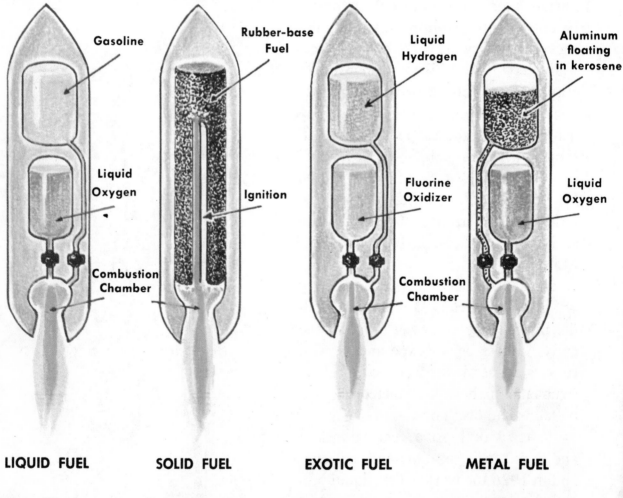

LIQUID FUEL

Specific Thrust: 264.
The liquid fuel flow is easy to control. The rocket design is complicated, and mechanical failures are apt to occur.

SOLID FUEL

Specific Thrust: Above 250.
Solid fuel is easily stored and handled, but fuel combustion is hard to control.

EXOTIC FUEL

Specific Thrust: 373.
Exotic fuel gives the rocket greater speed and larger load-carrying capacity, but is difficult to store and handle.

METAL FUEL

Specific Thrust: 325.
It is easily made and stored, but metal fuel is apt to clog pipelines. It is also hard to keep aluminum in suspension.

HOW IS A MULTI-STAGE MISSILE CONSTRUCTED?

IT WAS America's own Dr. Goddard who first discovered that by mounting one rocket atop another — automatically firing the next stage above when the first had burned out — speeds and distances could be achieved that were impossible with a single-stage rocket. In some instances, the instrument-carrying satellite has its own rocket engine which goes into orbit, too.

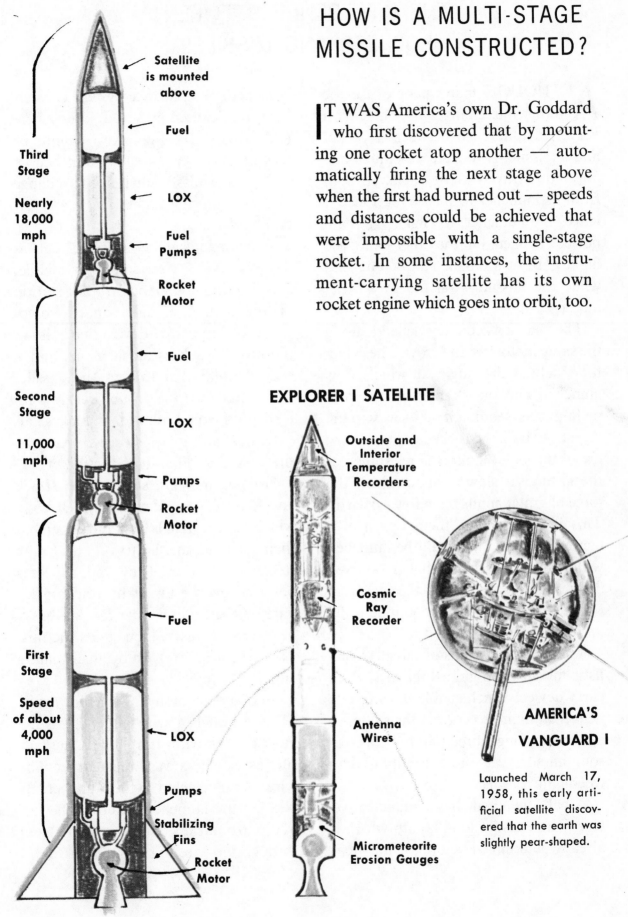

Third Stage

Nearly 18,000 mph

- Satellite is mounted above
- Fuel
- LOX
- Fuel Pumps
- Rocket Motor

Second Stage

11,000 mph

- Fuel
- LOX
- Pumps
- Rocket Motor

First Stage

Speed of about 4,000 mph

- Fuel
- LOX
- Pumps
- Stabilizing Fins
- Rocket Motor

EXPLORER I SATELLITE

- Outside and Interior Temperature Recorders
- Cosmic Ray Recorder
- Antenna Wires
- Micrometeorite Erosion Gauges

AMERICA'S VANGUARD I

Launched March 17, 1958, this early artificial satellite discovered that the earth was slightly pear-shaped.

5

THE DIFFERENCE BETWEEN
ROCKETS AND MISSILES

ALTHOUGH many people use the terms interchangeably, there is a very real difference between a rocket and a missile. A rocket, very much like an arrow, travels along a curved path from its launcher to the target. Once it leaves the launcher, its flight path cannot be changed. On the other hand, the flight path of a missile can be changed while the missile is on the way to its target.

The rocket's accuracy depends upon the same factors as an arrow. These factors include the angle at which it is launched and the strength of the propelling force sending it on its way to the target. As both the rocket and the arrow travel through the air, the resistance of the air tends to slow them down, and the force of gravity pulls them toward earth. This is what causes them to travel a curved path. If they could be launched with sufficient force so that the curved flight path was the same as the curvature of the earth, they would continue to fly and would, in effect, orbit it.

There are two kinds of missiles: ballistic missiles and guided missiles. Both carry devices which enable them to maneuver in flight, to correct their course, and even change direction. For this reason, missiles are more accurate than free-flight rockets.

A ballistic missile has a guidance system that sends it along a path which is already determined before the missile is launched. Its guidance system corrects for errors caused by speed, atmosphere and gravity. Its flight path cannot be changed once the missile is launched.

A guided missile can be told to change directions during flight. There are several kinds.

A command guided missile, such as the Army's *Nike* ground-to-air missile, gets steering commands from a station on the ground. Usually, that involves radar or some other device that follows the target, such as an airplane, and a second radar that follows the missile. A computer on the ground receives information from both radars, makes calculations, and issues steering orders to the missile to direct it to the target.

Homing missiles, such as the *Hawk* and *Redeye*, carry devices in their body which receive signals from the target and then steer the missile to it. The *Hawk* steers to the target by radar beams bounced off the target by tracking radars on the ground. The *Redeye* has a device in its nose which steers the missile to the heat given off by an airplane's engine.

Another common way to guide a missile is through a wire attached to the missile. Thin wires trail behind the missiles as they fly toward their target. The wires are connected to the launcher. By keeping the launcher aimed at the target, automatic corrections are sent through the wire to steer the missile.

HAWK • A two-stage, solid-propellant missile, *Hawk* can search out and destroy attacking aircraft. It can be airlifted by helicopter or medium-sized aircraft, and is capable of a high rate of fire.

WHEN WERE MISSILES FIRST USED
IN MODERN WARFARE?

THE FORMER dictator of Germany, Adolf Hitler, boasted he would win World War II with his "secret weapons." In the summer of 1944, unusual launching sites were observed along the Belgian and Dutch coasts by British airmen.

Soon after, these weapons — giant German V-2 missiles — began hurtling across the English Channel into London, the capital of England.

This ushered in an age of long-distance rocket-powered missiles that could carry nuclear warheads.

A V-2 LAUNCHING

WERE MANY MISSILES AND ROCKETS
USED IN WORLD WAR II?

ALTHOUGH the Germans had built and fired huge missiles into England, they spent little time or effort on smaller artillery-type rockets.

However, the Russians, invaded by Germany and desperate for increased firepower, perfected several types of barrage rockets.

The British used unguided rockets fired from airplanes as early as 1941.

And an American Army Lieutenant Colonel, Leslie A. Skinner, perfected the shoulder-fired anti-tank rocket, called the Bazooka, in 1942. It was used successfully in North Africa later that year.

Later, in the island battles of the Pacific, when U. S. Marines had gone ashore and the big guns and the air bombing had ceased, it was the rockets that gave support to the land forces.

HOW DOES A ROCKET WORK?

THE MIGHTY *Saturn 5* and the Fourth of July skyrocket have much in common. They both work on the same principle, relying for success on a law of motion discovered by Sir Isaac Newton, a brilliant mathematician and scientist. It states that *for every action, there is an equal and opposite reaction.* In other words, whenever a force exerts a push or a pull on an object in one direction (an action), the object itself exerts an equal push or pull in the opposite direction (a reaction). If you fire a gun, it moves backward — it recoils, or "kicks" — against your shoulder with a force equal to that of the bullet moving forward out of the gun barrel. The bullet moving forward is an action, and the gun moving backward is a reaction. As another example of Newton's reaction principle, if you jump forward off a scooter, the scooter itself moves backward. Your forward jump is the action; the scooter's move backward is the reaction. When burning gas rushes out of the rear of a rocket, it is an action whose reaction is the forward motion of the rocket. Tons of burning gas rush out of the rear of *Saturn 5* every second and give the rocket its 7½-million-pound thrust.

The burning gas is produced by ignited rocket fuel. There are two main types of rocket fuel: solid and liquid. Some solid fuels are black gunpowder, smokeless powder, and a chemical that is principally rubber. Among the liquid

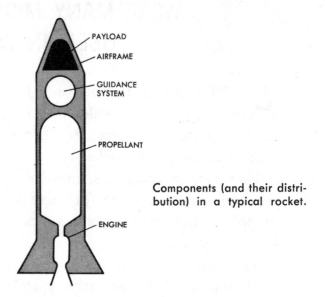

Components (and their distribution) in a typical rocket.

fuels in use are hydrogen peroxide (the same liquid that is a household antiseptic, only much more concentrated and purer), alcohol, gasoline, hydrogen, fluorine, and liquid oxygen. Rocket fuels are better termed rocket propellants.

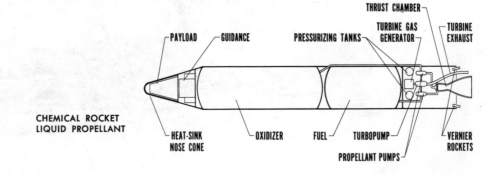

A solid propellant is the simplest in construction. The solid-propellant rocket engine need consist only of a place to burn the propellant (a combustion chamber), an exhaust nozzle at the rocket's rear, and a device to ignite the propellant. Liquid propellants are much more complicated to use than solid ones. The liquid-propellant rocket engine consists of at least two storage tanks, and pumps force the propellant through pipes to the combustion chamber. A power system for the pumps and many kinds of controls are also necessary parts of the liquid-propellant rocket. To compensate for a more complicated combustion system, though, a liquid-propellant rocket has certain advantages: it can be made more powerful than a solid-propellant engine; the thrust of the engine can be varied (a solid-propellant engine's thrust cannot); some liquid-propellant engines can be stopped and restarted while the rocket is in flight, whereas solid propellants can only be stopped and not restarted.

A large modern rocket with hundreds of thousands of parts and requiring dozens of men to launch it is not very much like a Fourth of July skyrocket ... yet there is no difference in the principle that moves either the huge rocket or the small one. It is Newton's fundamental reaction law that drives all rockets on their flights.

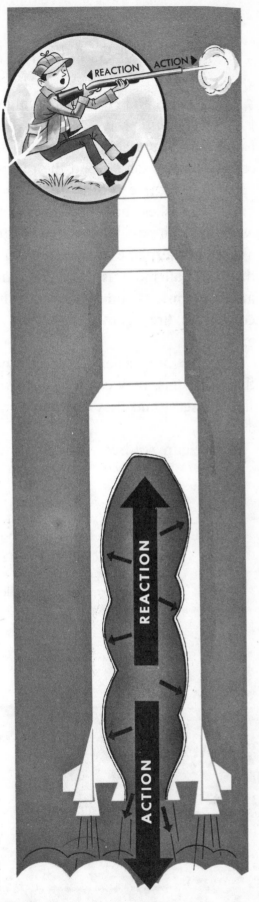

For every action, there is an equal and opposite reaction.

HOW DOES THE MODERN ARMY USE ROCKETS?

MISSILES and rockets are valuable weapons in the U.S. Army today. Long-range surface-to-surface missiles can hit targets far beyond the reach of cannon. A variety of ground-to-air guided missiles has been developed which make it possible to defend against all types of airplanes and even intercontinental ballistic missiles. The Army also uses missiles and rockets on its helicopters to fire against targets on the ground.

Missiles are easier to move about than are guns, they carry bigger explosive charges, and they are much more . accurate.

American soldiers also use much smaller missiles which they can carry on their backs and fire from foxholes. The *Dragon,* for example, weighs about 30 pounds and can knock out tanks as far away as 1,000 yards. The *Redeye,* which also weighs about 30 pounds, can be fired from the soldier's shoulder to knock down attacking airplanes.

One Army missile, the *Shillelagh,* is fired from the same tank gun that shoots conventional shells.

Army missiles are designed to be moved from place to place very quickly so that they can go anywhere the soldiers go on the battlefield. Most of them use solid-fuel rocket motors and can be ready to fire in seconds.

PERSHING • The Army's long-range missile, *Pershing,* can carry a nuclear warhead about 400 miles. It is a two-stage, solid-propellant ballistic missile.

LANCE • The *Lance* missile is about 20 feet long and weighs about 1 ½ tons. It is powered by pre-packaged storable liquid, and can be carried into combat by a helicopter.

TOW • The wire-guided *Tow* missile weighs only 60 pounds. Fired from helicopters, it is very effective against heavy tanks.

SHILLELAGH • *Shillelagh* is a 60-pound guided missile fired from armored combat vehicles. Its command guidance system makes it very accurate against moving or stationary targets.

WHAT TYPES OF MISSILES AND ROCKETS ARE SHOT FROM PLANES?

FIGHTER PLANES of the Navy, Air Force and Marines carry missiles which they fire at other airplanes from very long ranges. And there are other missiles that can be used for close-in dogfighting, such as the *Sidewinder* or *Sparrow*. The *Sidewinder* has a heat-seeking device that steers it to the target airplane engine. The *Sparrow* and the newer *Phoenix* missile are both radar-guided.

Army helicopters can now attack ground targets such as tanks, firing the wire-towed *Tow* missile, and will soon have the longer-range *Hellfire*, a missile guided by a laser beam.

The **SPARROW III** is a 12-foot rocket which rides a radar beam to the target. Used by both the U.S. Navy and the Marine Corps, it attains a speed of more than 1,500 mph within seconds after being fired from its fitting beneath a supersonic plane.

The **SIDEWINDER**, a solid-propellant rocket, is named after a fast and deadly rattlesnake. This rocket strikes fast and is infrared-guided to its target.

WHY ARE MISSILES USED AGAINST AIRPLANES?

MISSILES are very effective against modern high-speed airplanes whose great speed and maneuverability make them difficult to bring down. Missiles can engage airplanes at any altitude and can be fired in seconds. The Army's *Hawk*, a quick-firing, solid-propellant missile, is especially designed for use against low-flying, high-speed airplanes.

HOW DO MISSILES SHOOT DOWN OTHER MISSILES?

PROTECTING some of the United States' own intercontinental ballistic missiles, the U.S. Army Safeguard Ballistic Missile Defense System uses very complex radars, computers and high-speed missiles to defend against attack by intercontinental ballistic missiles.

The warhead of an intercontinental ballistic missile is very difficult to hit. Relatively small in size, it carries a thermonuclear device and arrives at a speed of more than 15,000 miles an hour. Even with long-range radars, the total time from initial detection to successful intercept is only a few seconds.

The Safeguard system uses two types of missiles. The big *Spartan* would be fired to intercept attacking missiles at long range. The much smaller *Sprint* would be used at short range. Both missiles are fired from below-ground launch cells. The solid-fuel rocket motors used in *Sprint* give it tremendous acceleration. The missile travels so fast that it must have special heat protection to keep it from burning up in the earth's atmosphere.

HOW WILL PERMANENT MISSILE BASES BE CONSTRUCTED FOR INSTANT USE AGAINST ENEMY ATTACK?

HIDDEN deep below the ground in concrete silos, intercontinental missiles stand ready for quick firing in the case of attack. Within an underground labyrinth, the missile battery control center has computers, fueling facilities, and supply and living quarters. When the alarm is sounded, concrete trap doors open and the missiles are brought above ground, their aim and range data already set. The Launch Officer can fire them singly or in salvos.

A. The underground nerve center of the missile battery

B. Fuel and final adjustments before raising the missile into firing position

C. The missile is elevated for launching

D. The blast-off for the target

E. A replacement missile is brought up from deep storage

HOW DOES THE UNITED STATES NAVY USE ROCKETS?

The TERRIER,
a two-stage missile,
is taking the place
of naval artillery.

AFTER the use of rockets toward the end of World War II, the U. S. Navy developed shipboard rocket weapons for shore support and as anti-aircraft missiles. Both the TERRIER, a needle-nose missile, and the TALOS, a long-range ramjet weapon which is boosted into the skies by a rocket, have guidance systems so uncannily accurate that targets can be spotted beyond the range of human vision and destroyed.

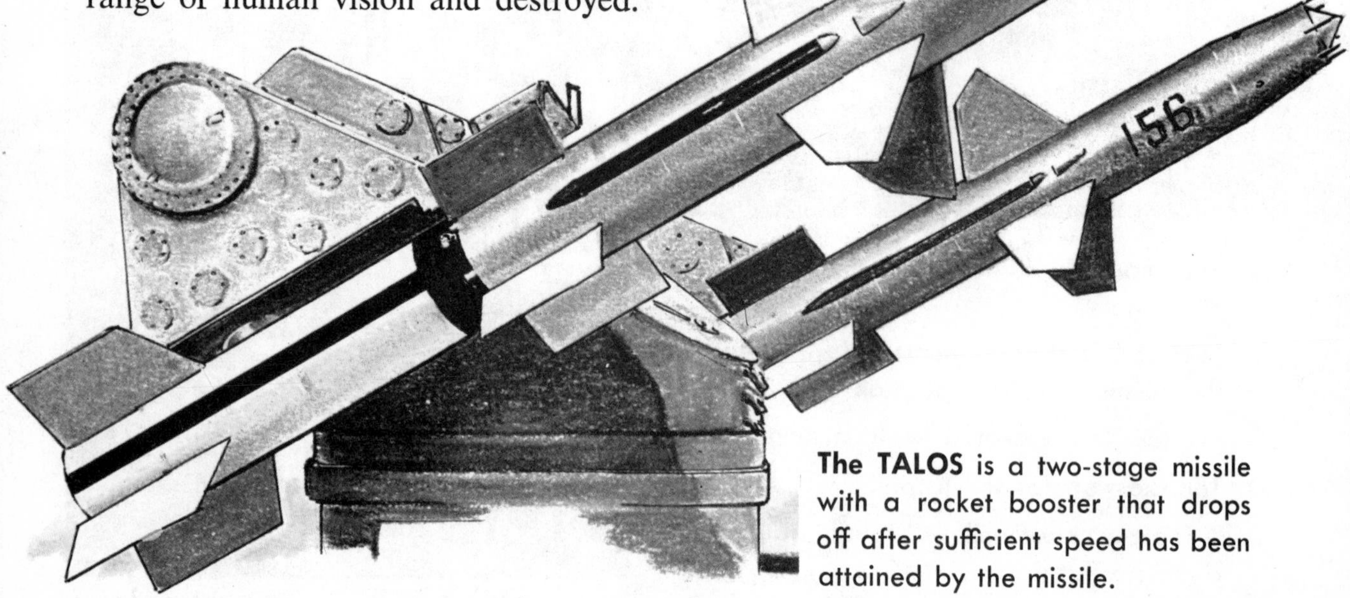

The TALOS is a two-stage missile with a rocket booster that drops off after sufficient speed has been attained by the missile.

HOW DOES THE UNITED STATES NAVY PLAN TO USE ROCKETS IN UNDERSEA WARFARE?

WHEN a lurking enemy submarine is located, surface ships can fire a RAT (rocket-assisted torpedo) toward the suspected area. The rocket hurls the torpedo in the direction of the

Rocket falls away

Parachute opens

Homing device finds target

target, a parachute lowers it into the water close by, and a homing device guides it to the kill.

The U.S. Navy's atomic submarines are capable of launching a salvo of *Polaris* missiles which can fly supersonically to a target 1,500 miles away.

The submarines can remain submerged far from land for weeks and, when the time comes to strike, can fire their missiles from the depths of the sea or from the surface.

The first successful firing of a ballistic missile from under water took place on July 20, 1960, when a POLARIS missile was fired from the nuclear submarine *George Washington*. At the time of the firing, the *George Washington* was submerged in 50 to 60 feet of water.

WHICH ARE THE UNITED STATES LONG-RANGE MISSILES?

Missile experiments in the United States got underway during World War II and continued afterward. It was particularly helpful in the early years following the war for U.S. military and industrial experts to examine and fire captured German V-2 missiles. Many of the German experts who designed and built the V-2 came to the United States after the war, worked for a time for the U.S. Army, and still play a key role in America's space program.

All U.S. military services developed long-range missiles to meet their particular needs. The first military long-range missiles were also modified and used to launch America's first space exploration missions, orbiting satellites, animals, and finally man.

TITAN II • A "heavyweight" ICBM, the *Titan II* plays a vital role in the U.S. Air Force deterrent force. It is launched directly from an underground storage silo.

PERSHING

Service Branch	U.S. Army
Height (feet)	35
Weight (pounds)	10,000
No. of stages	1
Range (miles)	400
Contractor(s)	Martin

POLARIS

Service Branch	U.S. Navy
Height (feet)	31
Weight (pounds)	30,000
No. of stages	1
Range (miles)	2,500
Contractor(s)	Lockheed

TITAN

Service Branch	U.S. Air Force
Height (feet)	103
Weight (pounds)	300,000
No. of stages	2
Range (miles)	5,000
Contractor(s)	Martin

SATURN 5

Service Branch	NASA
Height (feet)	278
Weight (pounds)	6,000,000
No. of stages	3
Range (miles)	—
Contractor(s)	Boeing/North American/ McDonnell-Douglas

HOW DO ROCKETS "BOOST" JET-PROPELLED MISSILES ON THEIR WAY TO A TARGET?

THE MACE, a pilotless jet-propelled missile with a nuclear warhead, was developed by the Air Force. It is typical of missiles boosted from zero-length launchers. Powerful winged rockets such as these can be hidden in wooded areas and fired at targets as far as 600 miles away.

Such missiles, and all equipment for firing them, can be flown to any part of the world aboard large cargo planes and can be ready for firing within hours.

To assist the MACE's jet engine on the take-off, a RATO unit is attached to the tail of the missile. This solid-propellant rocket booster gives it the necessary acceleration toward full flying speed. When this has been achieved and the booster is no longer needed, it falls away, while the MACE goes on alone.

WHAT RECORDS WERE MADE WITH AMERICA'S FIRST ROCKET PLANES?

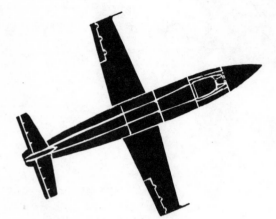

point at which it was feared the terrific speeds might melt the structure of the craft. Built of titanium (lighter than steel), it flew over 2,100 mph and in 1956 it climbed to 25 miles above the surface of the earth. Its rocket engines burned an alcohol-water mixture and used liquid oxygen as an oxidizer.

THE BELL X-1, piloted by Capt. Charles E. Yeager of the United States Air Force, was the world's first manned aircraft to fly faster than the speed of sound. It traveled at 1,650 mph and in 1954 reached an altitude of 17 miles.

Rocket-driven planes having broken the sound barrier, the X-2 was designed to probe the thermal barrier — that

The "X" series of rocket planes are built for research and carry fuel for no more than five minutes of powered flight. Carried aloft under the wing of a mother plane, they are released above 35,000 feet, where the rocket engines are ignited.

WHAT DOES THE X-15 ACCOMPLISH?

THE X-15, an experimental rocket plane, was developed for manned rocket research at the very edge of space, above 99.99 per cent of the earth's atmosphere. The X-15 carries out its research above the desert near

Edwards Air Force Base in California.

The X-15 is carried beneath the wing of a B-52 bomber to an altitude of between 40,000 to 50,000 feet, from where it is released. It plummets for 1,500 feet, and then its 600,000-horsepower engine ignites and burns for 90 seconds. The rocket plane flashes upward toward cislunar space. After the rocket has burned out, the X-15 still continues upward for thousands of feet and then arches downward, reentering the thicker atmosphere. It glides back to earth and, using skis instead of wheels, lands on the desert.

The X-15 has soared to 67 miles above the earth and has reached speeds of 4,534 miles per hour, nine times the speed of sound. The newest X-15 planes are designed to fly even higher, at speeds up to 5,300 miles per hour.

HOW FAST MUST A ROCKET TRAVEL TO ESCAPE EARTH'S GRAVITATIONAL PULL?

TO GO to the moon — our only natural satellite—a rocket missile must attain a speed of 25,000 mph to escape from the earth's pull. This must be done with multi-stage rockets, each individual stage sending the missile farther into space and at increasing speed.

When the last stage is fired, the missile must be traveling at seven miles per second. It is by this means that the *Apollo* astronauts are sent to the vicinity of the moon. A command module stays in orbit around the moon, while a lunar module descends to the surface.

Shown here are the space paths of a typical *Apollo* mission.

THE BEGINNING OF MANNED SPACE FLIGHT

BEFORE MAN became a passenger in spacecraft, scientists sent monkeys and dogs into space to see what effect the absence of gravity would have on them. The tests were successful, and manned flight followed shortly afterward.

PROJECT MERCURY:

Project *Mercury* was the United States' first manned space program. Its principal objective was to study man's ability to travel in space and return safely to earth.

On May 5, 1961, Navy Commander Alan B. Shephard, Jr., America's first astronaut, was launched into space in the *Mercury* capsule *Freedom 7* for a 15-minute, 115-mile-high suborbital flight. Another suborbital flight was made in *Liberty Bell 7* by Marine Captain Virgil I. ("Gus") Grissom. These successful flights were followed by four orbital flights by Project *Mercury* astronauts Marine Lt. Colonel John Glenn in *Friendship 7,* Lt. Commander Scott Carpenter in *Aurora 7,* Commander Walter M. Schirra, Jr. in *Sigma 7,* and finally Air Force Colonel L. Gordon Cooper, Jr. in *Faith 7.* Colonel Cooper orbited the earth 22 times in 34½ hours and traveled more than half a million miles.

The *Mercury* capsules were 7 feet in diameter at the base and 10 feet tall. They orbited between 100 and 150 miles above the earth. The capsule was slowed at reentry time by firing retrorockets.

RE-ENTERING THE EARTH'S ATMOSPHERE:

Returning to earth from space posed as great a problem as leaving for space. Scientists, designers, engineers, and countless technological experts worked for many years to overcome the problem of safe reentry. This was, in fact, one of the major problems to overcome in the early days of space exploration.

A spacecraft travels at thousands of miles an hour. When it enters the earth's atmosphere, friction causes intense heat, enough to melt the metal capsule. Consequently, it is necessary to retard or dissipate the heat; this is done by using special metals, insulation, and coating the capsule with ablative materials.

In returning from space missions, vehicles must also penetrate the atmosphere at the proper angle. If it reenters at too shallow an angle, the spacecraft could ricochet back into space. If it reenters at too steep an angle, it could burn up because of the excessive heat caused by friction.

THE SATURN 5:

The *Saturn 5* is the most powerful launch vehicle ever built. On its pad, fully assembled, with the *Apollo* spacecraft mounted on top, ready for a lunar launch, it is 363 feet tall. Loaded with fuel, it weighs 6 million pounds.

The *Saturn 5* is really made up of three separate rockets stacked one on top of another. Each of these stages is

APOLLO 16 LAUNCH

a complete rocket with its own engines and fuel tanks.

The largest and most powerful of these stages is the "booster." Its five engines give it a thrust of 7½ million pounds to lift it from the launch pad and start the entire vehicle on its journey into space. It is so large that it must be transported from its manufacturing plant to the launch site on a special ship.

The second stage is as big around as the first, but it is not as long. It, too, moves by water to the launch site. It has five engines, which add speed to the spacecraft after the booster stage has dropped away.

The third, or upper, stage is smaller than the others, but it is still quite large. A special airplane called the *Super Guppy* was built to transport it.

WHAT WAS THE FIRST UNITED STATES SATELLITE PUT INTO ORBIT AROUND THE EARTH?

ON January 31, 1958, a modified *Redstone* missile known as a Jupiter-C was launched from Cape Canaveral, Florida, carrying the man-made satellite *Explorer 1,* weighing 30.8 pounds. The first stage, an Army *Red-* *stone* missile, sent it sixty miles up. At 212 miles, a programmed maneuver tipped the vehicle to a course parallel with the earth. And six seconds later, the fourth-stage rockets rammed *Explorer 1* into orbit around the earth.

WHAT WAS EXPLORER 1'S IMPORTANT DISCOVERY?

THE most important discovery of the International Geophysical Year was made by *Explorer 1,* the first U.S. orbiting satellite. It confirmed what was then thought to be two belts of intense radiation surrounding the earth, except for areas over the North and South Poles. One apparently existed about 3,500 miles beyond our atmo- sphere, and the other existed at a distance between 8,000 and 12,000 miles.

A physicist named James A. Van Allen is credited with the identification of these radiation belts, and thus they were named for him.

Later discoveries by means of space probes in 1962 caused scientists to revise their beliefs regarding the radiation

The tall structure at the left, used to fuel and service each separate stage of the missile, is rolled back before the firing takes place.

belts. Now they are of the opinion that only one large belt exists, one extending outward about 40,000 miles from earth, beginning approximately five hundred miles about the equator. The Van Allen Radiation Belt appears to consist of protons and electrons trapped in the earth's magnetic field.

Jupiter is another planet said to have such a radiation belt surrounding it.

WHY MUST ROCKETS BE USED FOR TRAVEL IN OUTER SPACE?

BEYOND the ionosphere, extending about three hundred miles above the earth, is the exosphere, the uppermost layer of our atmosphere which contains almost no air molecules. Long before this point is reached, piston and jet engines would become inoperative, since they must draw in sufficient air to mix with the fuel they use.

It was the American rocket scientist, Robbert Goddard who first proved, both mathematically and by actual test, that a rocket will work in a vacuum. Its fuel, when mixed with liquid oxygen (often called LOX) in the firing chamber, will explode and burn, creating *thrust*. Therefore, the rocket engine is unlike any other in that it carries its own "air" with it.

Another of its advantages for manned space travel is that its speed of acceleration can be so controlled by the flow of fuel, that the initial "blast-off" from the ground can be kept at speeds man can stand.

This four-barreled rocket engine, weighing only 210 pounds, produced 6,000 pounds of *thrust*. It pushed the X-1 through the sonic barrier to a height of 90,000 feet.

HOW ARE MISSILES MOVED AND FIRED?

U.S. AIR FORCE intercontinental ballistic missiles are stored and fired from underground launchers called "silos." Air Force, Navy and Marine fighter planes carry missiles and rockets on mounts beneath their wings. U.S. Navy ground-to-air missiles are fired from mounts on ships and stored in special areas called "magazines" below deck. Submarine-launched missiles are carried and fired from special launchers built into the submarine.

U.S. Army missiles must go where the soldier goes, fight where he fights. Some, like *Dragon* and *Redeye,* are designed to be carried on the soldier's back. The missile carrying case serves as a launcher.

Larger surface-to-surface missiles, such as *Lance* and *Pershing,* are moved and fired from special vehicles. The *Lance* transporter has tracks instead of wheels and can travel almost anywhere. It can even cross rivers or be parachuted from airplanes. The big *Pershing* missile is moved and fired from a towed launcher that looks very much like a flatbed tractor-trailer truck.

Army ground-to-air missiles such as *Hawk* can be fired from tracked transports or set up in semi-permanent mounts around a place to be defended, such as an airfield.

All of them can be ready to fire in seconds and need only a few technicians to operate.

HELLFIRE • Launched from attack helicopters, *Hellfire* is laser-guided, and is being developed for use against a variety of targets, including anti-aircraft guns.

SAM-D • A highly mobile system, mounted on wheeled vehicles, *SAM-D* is a solid-propellant, single-stage missile used against high performance aircraft.

STINGER • As mobile as a man, the 35-pound *Stinger* is a lethal weapon against helicopters, observation aircraft, and transport planes.

WHERE DO WE STAND IN SPACE ACCOMPLISHMENTS?

THE SPACE AGE opened when the U.S.S.R. launched the first artificial (man-made) satellite, *Sputnik 1*. Since then a staggering amount of effort and money has been expended in the interest of space exploration and of learning more about the vast universe.

Spacecraft have been launched by many nations, but mostly by the United States and the Soviet Union. They have been of many different kinds. The greatest number have been earth-orbiting artificial satellites which have measured the earth's magnetic field, its radiation field, its shape, and its size. Other satellites have photographed clouds, sending back to earth hundreds of pictures every day of the year, enabling meteorologists to predict weather more accurately than they have ever done. They have measured the water vapor, ozone, and temperature of the atmosphere. Other satellites transmit signals as an aid to navigators, and still others transmit messages and television pictures for instant communication.

Before man himself went to the moon, unmanned space vehicles were sent ahead. They orbited the moon, crash-landed and soft-landed on its surface, and took thousands of photographs. The far side of the moon, hidden from the sight of man for eons, was revealed at last. Later, the moon's dust-

(Opposite page) The earth, home planet of all mankind, seen from a distance of approximately 98,000 miles.

One of the first living space travellers was a dog; it was a passenger in a Russian spacecraft, Sputnik II (October, 1957).

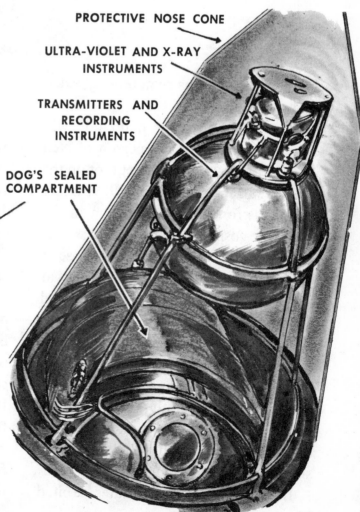

PROTECTIVE NOSE CONE

ULTRA-VIOLET AND X-RAY INSTRUMENTS

TRANSMITTERS AND RECORDING INSTRUMENTS

DOG'S SEALED COMPARTMENT

like "soil" itself was remotely collected and analyzed.

"One giant leap for mankind" was achieved as man, in the person of Neil A. Armstrong, physically set foot on the moon's surface on July 20, 1969. Other *Apollo* astronauts followed him in the quest for cosmic knowledge.

Space probes have journeyed close to the sun to gain information about that huge astronomical body. Venus and Mars have been visited by instrumented spacecraft and their secrets are slowly being disclosed. We now know for certain that Venus, with a surface temperature of approximately 800° F., could not sustain the life of any known animal or plant. And Mars has meteor craters similar to those on the moon.

In 1973, the United States orbited a space station called *Skylab*. It was a large and comfortable home and scientific laboratory in space where three-man crews lived and worked for periods of 28, 59, and 84 days. Orbiting at an altitude of 270 miles above the earth, they made important discoveries about the sun, the earth, and the universe.

Now that *Skylab* has shown the way, various space stations will in time be assembled to serve the needs of science. Man has demonstrated his capability to live and work in space for long periods of time. Periodically the space stations could be restocked with provisions and fuel — and relief crews could be sent up from earth. Celestial observations, especially, will be improved tremendously from such vantage points outside the interference of the earth's atmosphere.

WHAT DANGERS DOES MAN FACE IN OUTER SPACE?

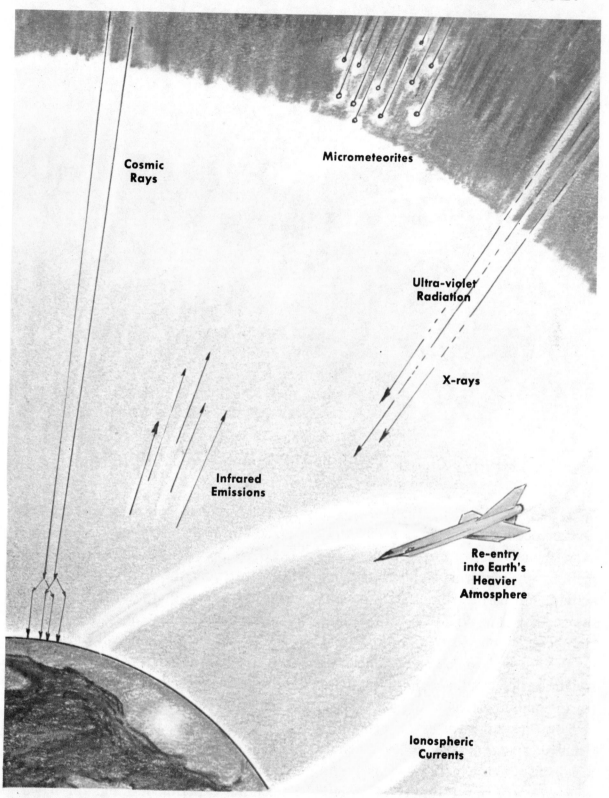

Cosmic Rays

Micrometeorites

Ultra-violet Radiation

X-rays

Infrared Emissions

Re-entry into Earth's Heavier Atmosphere

Ionospheric Currents

THE *Apollo* flights to the moon supplied first-hand knowledge of the effects upon man as he explored the lunar surface. But future astronauts will encounter more hazards as they travel greater distances in space. The risks must be lessened and countless problems must be overcome, just as they were by the flights that preceded the moon landings.

SPACE SHUTTLE VEHICLE

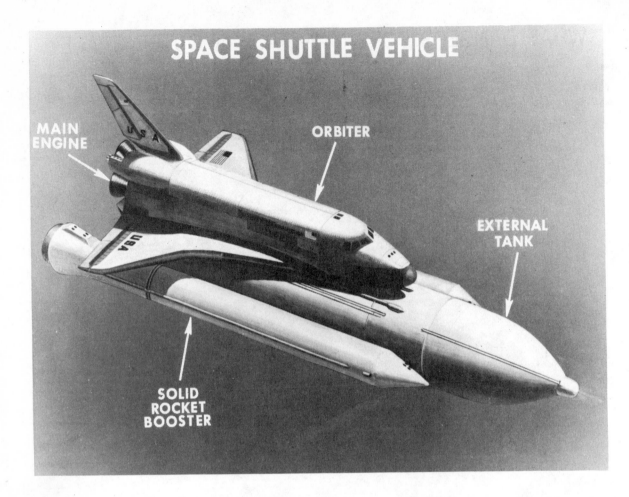

MAIN ENGINE

ORBITER

EXTERNAL TANK

SOLID ROCKET BOOSTER

THE NEXT ERA IN MANNED SPACE FLIGHT

THE MANNED space flight program has been evolutionary. First *Mercury,* then *Gemini,* proved human capability to perform highly technical activities in earth orbit. Later, *Apollo* showed that man could visit other planets. *Skylab* conclusively showed that man can adapt to the environment of weightlessness, and live and work there for indefinite periods.

Now the emphasis is on economy. The *Space Shuttle* is being developed as a vehicle which can be used over and over to carry out a variety of assignments in space. It will consist of an *Orbiter* vehicle, which is essentially a rocket-propelled airplane. The orbiter will "sit piggyback" on top of a large tank carrying the fuel, and two solid rocket boosters that launch it. When no longer needed, the tank and boosters will be discarded, and will burn up as they reenter the earth's atmosphere. The *Orbiter* will continue its space mission, then return and land like an airplane.

The *Space Shuttle* can be used to take satellites into orbit, to ferry crews to repair orbiting craft, to perform many scientific experiments, and for a variety of other missions.

The *Space Shuttle* will be launched from Kennedy Space Center in Florida, as were the *Saturn* launch vehicles. It will be launched in the vertical position, like a missile, but the *Orbiter* will return and land at the Space Center like an airplane.

Astronauts working in space outside moving space vehicles.

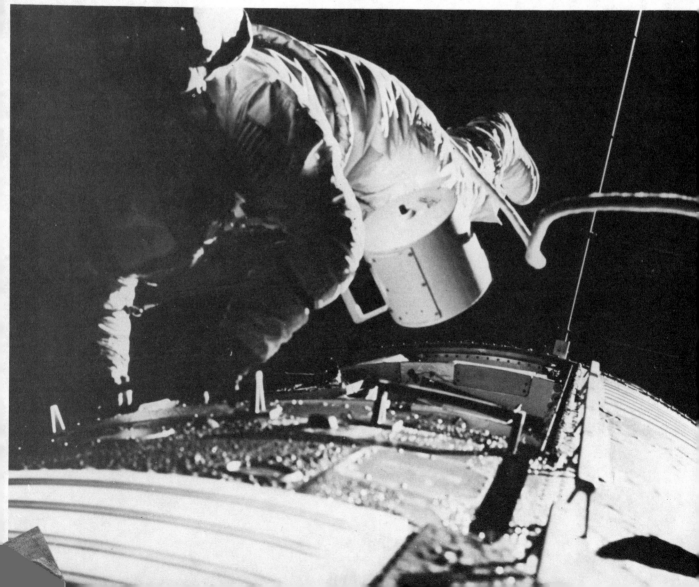

HOW MUST MAN BE PROTECTED
IN SPACE VEHICLES?

ON TRIPS to the moon and beyond, men must carry with them a supply of oxygen, food and liquid sufficient to last until their return to earth. They must be protected against intense heat and cold, the vacuum of space, and radiation from the sun and from outside the solar system (which includes electrons, protons and high-energy gamma rays). Meteors, even tiny ones, though not considered a major danger because of their comparative scarcity in relation to a given course, could conceivably penetrate a steel spacecraft and jeopardize the mission and the lives of the crew. Weightlessness in space, periods of complete inactivity, rapid acceleration and deceleration, confinement to close quarters, the problems of swallowing and the elimination of body waste—these are conditions which prevail and to which the men must adjust.

WHERE MIGHT MAN GO, AFTER THE MOON?

THE EARTH is a small planet among billions of stars and other celestial bodies in a universe that extends beyond man's imagination. A true star is any heavenly body like our sun, which is self-luminous; planets and satellites shine by reflected light. The solar system to which the earth belongs is made up of nine planets which revolve around the sun. Satellites, like the moon which orbits around the earth, circle around the planets. Our solar system is only a tiny part of a larger galaxy of stars — the Milky Way — and astronomers have discovered about a hundred million such galaxies, each of which may contain a hundred thousand planets.

It seems likely that somewhere among these billions of heavenly bodies, living conditions suitable to man may be present. He has thrived on earth because of a combination of elements: a deep band of atmosphere, water to drink, and heat for warmth and cooking.

Among the planets and satellites of our solar system, many are too hot or too cold to support human life, while others give off chemical fumes that would destroy it. Only Mars, from present indications, might serve as a base of operations, provided man takes his own "atmosphere" along.

HOW FAR AWAY ARE OTHER PLANETS IN OUR SOLAR SYSTEM?

Planet	Mean Distance from Sun (Millions of Miles)	Length of Year	Period of Rotation	Diameter (Miles)	Gravity at Surface (Earth=1)
Mercury	36	88 days	88 days	3,000	0.27
Venus	67.2	225 days	Unknown	7,600	0.85
Earth	93	365 days	1 day	7,920	1.00
Mars	141.5	687 days	24.6 hours	4,220	0.38
Jupiter	483.3	11.86 years	9.9 hours	89,000	2.64
Saturn	886	29.46 years	10.2 hours	75,000	1.17
Uranus	1,783	84 years	10.7 hours	31,000	0.92
Neptune	2,793	164.8 years	15.8 hours	28,000	1.12
Pluto	3,675	248.4 years	Unknown	6,300	Unknown

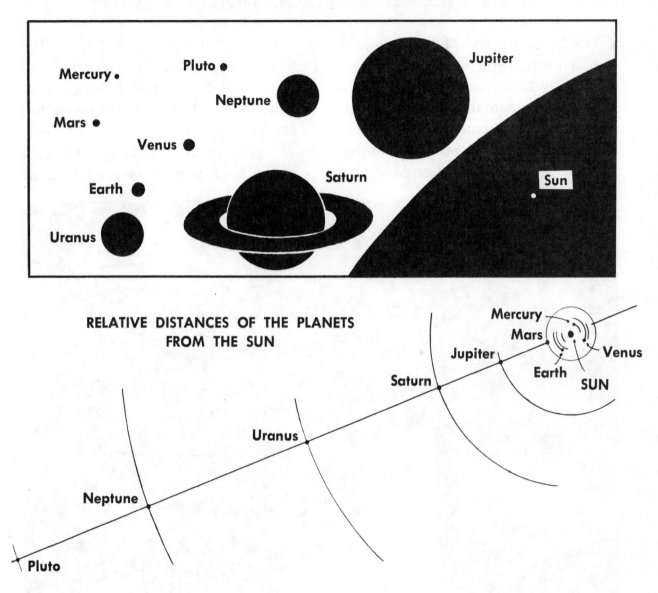

RELATIVE DISTANCES OF THE PLANETS FROM THE SUN

THE SATELLITES OF THE PLANETS

MARS: 2 satellites. Diameters: 5 and 1 miles. Orbits: 3,700 and 14,500 miles. Circuit time: ½ and 1½ days.

JUPITER: 13 satellites. Diameters: 3 to 3,200 miles. Orbits: 112,600 to 14,888,000 miles. Circuit time: ½ to 760 days.

SATURN: 9 satellites. Diameters: 200 to 3,550 miles. Orbits: 115,000 to 8,034,000 miles. Circuit time: 1 to 550 days.

URANUS: 5 satellites. Diameters: 150 to 1,000 miles. Orbits: 80,800 to 364,000 miles. Circuit time: 1½ to 13½ days.

NEPTUNE: 2 satellites. Diameters: 200 and 3,000 miles. Orbits: 220,000 and 5,000,000 miles. Circuit time: 6 and 730 days.

WHEN WILL TRUE SPACE TRAVEL BEGIN?

CLOSE to the end of the twentieth century, people so inclined may be able to fly to a lunar-orbiting station and view the mountains of the moon. At least, that is what some people envision. By that time, too, it is possible that the first men will have landed on Mars.

Such predictions, while "out of this world," are no longer considered outlandish. Not since that historic day in July, 1969, when Neil Armstrong first stepped onto the moon. The *Space Shuttle* will make routine space travel a reality. So, real space travel is not far off.

In the future, manned space stations orbiting around the earth may be visited regularly by shuttle-craft with supplies and men.

THE HOW AND WHY WONDER BOOK OF
ATOMIC ENERGY

Written by DONALD BARR
Assistant Dean, School of Engineering
Columbia University

Illustrated by GEORGE J. ZAFFO

Editorial Production: DONALD D. WOLF

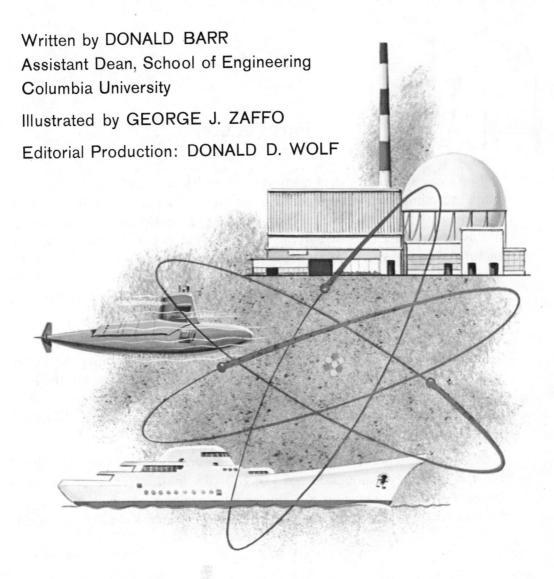

Edited under the supervision of
Dr. Paul E. Blackwood
Washington, D. C.

Text and illustrations approved by
Oakes A. White, Brooklyn Children's Museum, Brooklyn, New York

GROSSET & DUNLAP • Publishers • NEW YORK

Introduction

Big ideas sometimes deal with very small things, and small things are often exceedingly important. Witness the atom. Scientists have had some of their biggest ideas about these tiny particles of matter. Their ideas about atoms have changed as discoveries have brought new information into the picture. *The How and Why Wonder Book of Atomic Energy* takes the science-minded reader along the exciting road of discovery about the atom that led to the first use of atomic energy in a controlled way, and tells how people from many countries made scientific contributions.

The life-blood of scientific activity is in exploring all parts of the universe — even the tiny parts represented by atoms — and explaining the events that take place. Though individual atoms cannot be seen, they are the basis of all matter. And in the search for more information about atoms, scientists gradually came upon new knowledge about the energy within. This book tells this wonderful story.

Parents and schools will want to place *The How and Why Wonder Book of Atomic Energy* alongside the other books in this series. It not only brings the young reader up to date on the development of atomic energy, but challenges one to think about the yet-to-come atomic age of the future.

Paul E. Blackwood

Dr. Blackwood is a professional employee in the U. S. Office of Education. This book was edited by him in his private capacity and no official support or endorsement by the Office of Education is intended or should be inferred.

Library of Congress Catalog Card Number: 67-24093

1983 PRINTING

Contents

An atomic bomb destroyed Hiroshima.

A B-29 bomber dropped
the first wartime A-bomb.

The Atomic Age Begins

At 8:15 in the morning, on August
6, 1945, people in the Japanese city of
Hiroshima were getting out of bed, eat-
ing breakfast, beginning the day's work.
Japan was at war. Nazi Germany's terrible clanking armies had been beaten,
and the madman Hitler who had mur-
dered whole countries was dead. The
dictator Mussolini was dead, too, and
Italy had gone over to the other side.
The Japanese empire, which had started
out to conquer the whole world with
those partners, was now left to face the
United States and her allies alone. General MacArthur's armies were already

5

shooting and slashing their way into the islands that guarded Japan. For weeks American planes had rained fire bombs on Japanese cities. Thus far, Hiroshima had been spared. Then a lone American plane streaked over the city. It dropped one bomb. The Atomic Age had begun.

DEATH OF A CITY

There was a vast flash of fire, brighter than the sun, and hotter. There was a great shuddering of the earth and a great roar and a scorching wind. There was a cloud shaped like a huge mushroom, silently standing above the ruins. There was nothing left of the center of Hiroshima except charred, dusty rubbish from which deadly invisible rays were streaming. There were 78,150 people known to be dead and 13,983 people missing. From one bomb!

The President of the United States, Harry S. Truman, broadcast a warning to Japan. This, he said, was a new kind of bomb, a bomb which used the forces that made the sun hot, and America had more of these bombs. The President was slightly wrong in his science. But that did not matter. The Japanese knew that there *was* a new force in the world, and soon they surrendered.

On that August day, in laboratories all over the United States, scientists shivered and looked grim. That was not the way they had wanted the Atomic Age to begin.

The first atomic explosion on earth occurred in the New Mexico desert near Alamogordo in July, 1945.

Dawn in the Desert

Let us go back three weeks. It is a little before 3:00 o'clock in the morning on July 16, 1945. The rain is pouring down and the lightning is wildly stabbing the clouds over a lonely corner of Alamogordo Air Base in the New Mexico desert. It is not deserted tonight.

Men are scurrying through the darkness. There are soldiers, some of them wearing generals' stars. There are quiet men in business suits, whom the others address respectfully as "Professor." Between the crashes of thunder, they talk in little groups nervously. They go into a shed to examine some wires and instruments and drive away. Some go to another blockhouse a few miles away. Some drive six miles through the storm

and climb a tall steel tower to peer at a bulky, strange device nestling there among more wires and instruments. This is the device which is to be tested — an atomic device. It is known simply as "Fat Man." The men keep looking at the sky.

ZERO HOUR

At 3:30 there is a decision. Fat Man will be tested. At 4:00 o'clock the rain stops, but the clouds are thick overhead. By 5:10, the men have all gathered in the blockhouses. A voice crackles from the loudspeakers: "Zero minus twenty minutes." Men are rubbing suntan lotion on their faces and arms. The talking dies down. Some of the men are

praying. In one shed, when zero minus two is called, everyone lies on the floor, face down, with his feet pointing to the tower several miles away. In the other shed, the civilian scientist in charge of the project, Dr. J. Robert Oppenheimer, is hardly breathing. He holds onto a post to steady himself. At zero minus forty-five seconds, the automatic timers click on. The red hand glides around the clock face. Then the announcer yells, "Now!"

A blazing flash from the tower lights up the face of the desert and the mountains around it. There is an earsplitting roar which goes on and on. A blast of air knocks down two men who have stayed outside one of the sheds. An enormous, many-colored cloud boils up and up until it is eight miles tall. As it rises, the storm-clouds seem to move aside for it.

In the two sheds, the stiff faces have eased into smiles. Everyone is shaking everyone else's hand. There are shouts of laughter. A distinguished chemistry professor from Massachusetts throws his arms around Dr. Oppenheimer. "We did it! We did it!"

Fat Man has passed the test. The first atomic explosion on earth has just taken place.

A Dangerous Game

Let us go back two and a half years. It is mid-morning in Chicago, December 2, 1942. For a long time the University of Chicago has not played any football in its stadium, Stagg Field. It is a pity to waste the place. Under the grandstands there are rooms and courts for playing other games, and something is certainly going on in a squash court under the West Stands. But this is not squash, which is played with a rubber ball and rackets. This game is played with balls and rackets too small to see — hundreds of millions of them. The players can get hurt.

Above one end of the court is a balcony. Toward the other end, there is a monstrous black pile of something. It is strange-looking stuff, yet it somehow seems familiar. It is not metal, yet it is shiny, even a little greasy-looking. Where have we seen it before? In a pencil.

The "lead" in a pencil is not lead at all, but a form of carbon called *graphite*. Carbon comes in many forms, including coal and diamonds, but graphite is best for playing the atomic game. It can be sawed into neat shapes like wood. It can be made very pure. It is not rare.

FIFTY-TWO TONS OF URANIUM

This pile is made of neatly sawed bricks, stacked crisscross. It is very pure — or the players in the squash court hope it is — because if it isn't, something might go terribly wrong. And there are 1,350 tons of graphite in the court, piled 30 feet wide, 32 feet long, 21½ feet high. Some of the bricks in the middle of the stack have holes drilled in them. In these holes are lumps of a strange, rare metal called *uranium*. Almost all the uranium metal in the United States of America — fifty-two

tons of it — is here, buried in the big black pile under the seats at the football field. Also buried in the pile are 14,500 lumps of other stuff that has uranium in it.

Other holes have been drilled through the stacked graphite bricks. Lying in these are long rods of another rare metal, called *cadmium*. What the strange uranium can do, the strange cadmium can stop — the players hope.

For this game has never been played before, not since the creation of the earth. As the cadmium rods are pulled out of the pile, millions of tiny "balls" — much too small to see, even with a microscope — will shoot out of the uranium lumps. They will go right through the graphite and hit nearby uranium lumps, knocking more tiny balls out of them. These, too, will begin flying around and knocking more balls into the game. And the uranium and graphite will get hotter and hotter and hotter, like a furnace.

WILL IT WORK?

Now if the players are wrong, either of two things might happen. One is — nothing. There may not be enough balls, or they may not shoot through the graphite. Three years of hard work and millions and millions of dollars would be wasted. The other thing that might happen is — an explosion. There may be too many balls. The "furnace" may get too hot. And if it does, it could blow up not only the players and the squash court and the football field, but Chicago, Illinois.

The first atomic reactor, at Stagg Field in Chicago, Illinois, was a huge stack of carbon bricks. The central bricks had holes with lumps of uranium in them. Other holes were drilled through the stack for the cadmium "control rods," shown in diagram below.

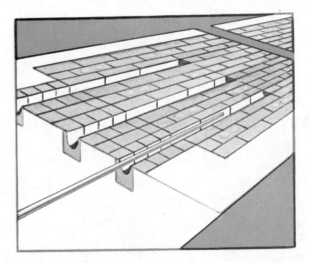

Now the players are ready. The captain of the team is an Italian-born scientist named Enrico Fermi. He invented the game. He has come from Columbia University in New York, a thousand miles away, to play. One of the players has his hand on a cadmium rod, waiting for the captain's signal to start the game. Three players are standing on top of the pile with big pails of water in their hands. The water has cadmium in it. If the game gets too "hot," they will douse it with the cadmium water before it blows up — *if* they have time. The scorekeeper is sitting at a cabinet covered with dials, like the dashboard of a car multiplied by ten. The dials tell him how many balls are flying, how hot the pile is getting. He will try to cry out a warning if the game goes wrong.

9

Fermi is sure it will not go wrong, and he is a world-famous physicist. He has checked his plans and calculations over and over again. He has checked them this morning. He does not think he will be like Mrs. Murphy's cow, which kicked over a lantern and started the Great Chicago Fire.

THE GAME STARTS

He gives the signal. A cadmium rod is pulled out. Another. All but one. The scorekeeper reports that the game is under way inside the great black heap.

The player takes the last cadmium rod and slowly pulls it out one foot. The scorekeeper's instruments click out the news — the pile is warming. It steadies, as Fermi's calculations said it would, before it gets really hot. The player pulls the rod out a little more. Then a pause. Check the instruments. Check the calculations. A little more. Check. A little more. Inch by inch.

It is lunchtime. Professor Fermi and his team go out to eat. After lunch, they inch the last cadmium rod out of the pile. At 3:25 P.M. the instruments have news. The pile has "gone critical" — it is hot — it is working.

Will it go too far, get too hot, explode? The clocks tick away the minutes. Still safe. At 3:53 P.M., Fermi tells the player with the rods to put them back. The game is over.

It is won. Man has built an atomic furnace. It can make electricity to light houses and run factories. It can make medicine to cure diseases. And it can make terrible explosives capable of killing thousands of people in a second.

One of the players reaches into his

Science has learned to use the energy of the atom for homes, factories, submarines, surface ships and medicine.

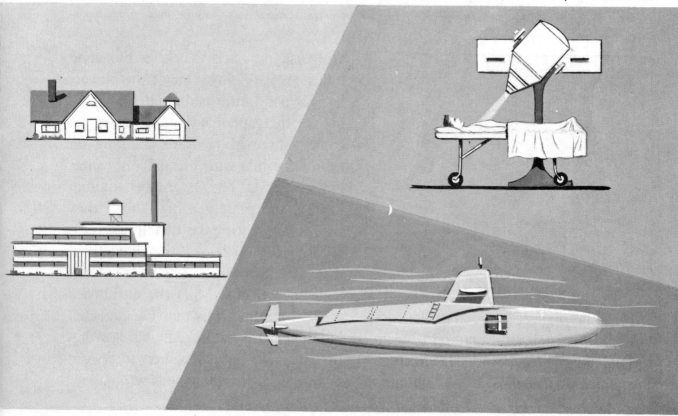

luggage and pulls out a bottle of Italian red wine. Fermi sends for paper cups. The members of the team hold their cups up — "Here's to the Atomic Age!"

A Little Extra Work

Let us go back four years. It is the evening of January 25, 1939, a cold, blowy evening in New York City. In a small, messy room in a basement at Columbia University, three men are working late.

For young Professor Dunning, it has been a busy day, and there is a lot more to do. He had lunch today with his friend Professor Fermi, who told him some exciting news. The news came in

tomic power can also
e used destructively.

a roundabout way, from Berlin, Germany.

Events have happened swiftly. Both Germany and Austria are now being ruled by a ruthless dictator named Adolf Hitler. Thousands of people have been brutally beaten, robbed of their possessions, or shot because the *Fuhrer* of the Third Reich (the title Hitler assumed) did not approve of their religion or political beliefs. Of the many citizens who are now seeking exile, one is Dr. Lise Meitner, an important woman physicist from Austria.

LETTER FROM BERLIN

A few weeks ago she got a letter from Otto Hahn, a chemist who has stayed in Germany. He said he had been experimenting with some uranium and discovered a strange thing — some of it had turned into another metal entirely. He hardly dared think what that meant. As soon as she read this, Dr. Meitner saw what it meant. She talked it over with friends in Denmark. One was Niels Bohr, who is the world's greatest expert on atoms. And Bohr was just leaving for a visit to America.

A few days ago he arrived and told some American scientists he was going to give a report on this new discovery to a meeting in Washington, tomorrow, January 26. The news has been spreading fast. Fermi talked it over with Dunning at lunch today, and then left for Washington to attend the meeting.

Young John Dunning, too, sees what it means. He sees that if you really do to uranium what Otto Hahn says he did to uranium, little bits of stuff will shoot

11

out of it — little balls too small to see, even with a microscope. And there will be sparks or flashes of energy — too small to see or feel. So all afternoon he has been trying to get equipment set up for a wonderful experiment. He is going to do what the German chemist did, and he is going to prove that the little bits of stuff really do fly off, and he is going to measure the energy. . . .

A SOUND NOBODY EVER HEARD

Dunning has clever hands. He has a way with gadgets. Here are some chunks of lead like children's blocks, and some chemicals and pipe and a lot of wire and some radio tubes and a

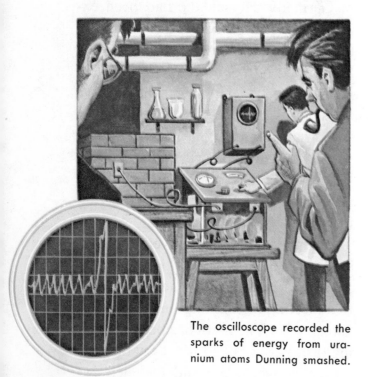

The oscilloscope recorded the sparks of energy from uranium atoms Dunning smashed.

small metal case with a round glass screen in one end. This is the equipment. It looks pretty sloppy, but it will work. It will do three things. It will

change the uranium. It will detect any flying bits of stuff or sparks of energy. And each time anything is detected, it will send an electric current into the thing that looks like a toy television set.

Two scientists who are working with him have come. Everything is ready. Dunning turns a switch on the case with the window. A glowing green line appears across it. He switches on the rest of the equipment. The green line becomes wiggly, almost furry. And then it happens.

A long green streak shoots up from the furry line. Blip! The signal. A second later, another. Blip! Blip-blip! Blip! Blip-blip-blip . . .

The three men are looking at atomic energy.

A Very Strange Idea

The whole universe — the great flaming stars scattered over billions of billions of miles, the earth under our feet, the air we breathe, the light we see by, the mysterious tiny blood cells flowing through our veins — all of this is made of only two kinds of things. One is *matter*. The other is *energy*.

What is the universe made of?

Though men have been living on earth for many thousands of years, it was not until the beginning of the twentieth century that they began to discover the relationship of matter and energy.

You may at one time or another have had the experience, for example, of staring at a word on a printed page —

12

an ordinary word which you may have seen hundreds of times — and suddenly feeling, after concentrating on it for a few minutes, that it was somehow "wrong." The longer you looked at the individual letters, the stranger the word may have seemed. You could even begin to convince yourself that the word was misspelled.

The same situation crops up in physics. As we study the whole page of the universe, the complicated events become essentially simple, but when concentrating upon the simple words on that page, they become unfamiliar.

What is the difference between matter and energy?

At first glance it looks as if matter and energy are quite different — matter weighs something and energy does not. However, since the year 1900, physicists have been giving this question a second, third and fourth glance. They have been puzzled by the fact that energy often acts like matter and matter acts like energy.

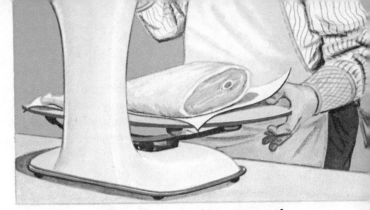

Mass is the amount of matter in a thing — meat, for example. One way to measure mass is with a scale.

But that's not always easy. The air above this scale has one ton of mass. Why doesn't what you see here take place?

Answer: Because the air also gets underneath the scale and pushes upward, just like water under a rowboat.

Another way to measure the mass of a thing is by the kind of wallop it gives when it hits you head-on.

FORE!

To the physicist, the word "work" means anything that uses energy — whether it's electricity, sunlight, chemical energy in food or rocket fuel, muscle exercise. Even watching T.V. or sunbathing takes work.

1 ERG = $\frac{1}{10,000,000}$ JOULES

1 HORSEPOWER UNIT = 1,980,000 FOOT-POUNDS

1 BRITISH THERMAL UNIT = .0002930 KILOWATT-HOURS

1 LARGE CALORIE = 2,087 FOOT-POUNDS

1 ERG = $\frac{1}{10,000,000}$ JOULES

The paper this book is printed on is matter, and it seems fairly solid and not particularly strange. It weighs something in your hand. Blow against it. It moves a little. Blow harder. It moves more. It has what physicists call *mass*.

The breath you blow against the book is not solid like the book, and at the moment you cannot tell that it weighs anything. There are several hundred miles of air piled on top of you, and yet you are not crushed. But a second's thought tells you that, although the matter in your breath is much more loosely arranged than the matter in the book, it has body to it, for when you blow up a balloon, you can feel the air

14

hard and long, using the marvelous electronic and magnetic eyes that science has invented, it begins to look very strange. It does look almost like a queer kind of thickened-up or frozen energy.

inside. And air actually weighs quite a lot. For a blimp, carrying crew and engines and fuel, floats in the sky by weighing a little less than air, just as a submarine floats in the sea by weighing a little less than water. So even very thinned-out matter has mass.

But the light by which you are reading this book is something

How can we tell matter from energy? else. It does not seem to weigh anything. You can shine a flashlight beam into a balloon and the balloon will not fill. If you blow sideways against the beam, it will not shift. Light does not seem to have any mass. It is not thinned-out matter, but energy.

Yet, when we stare at matter very

We still do not know very clearly what

What is energy? energy is. But we know what it does. It does *work*. Technically, we say that work is the applying of a force over a distance. More simply, it is the use of energy to move things or to change things. Work may be moving pieces of matter around — lifting a girder up the skeleton of a skyscraper, drilling a hole in the earth, hammering a nail, weaving cloth. Work may be changing the insides of matter — refining iron ore into iron metal, changing iron to steel in an open-hearth furnace, using derivatives of coal, air and water to make material called nylon. Work may be magnetizing and demagnetizing something, as happens thou-

15

Energy is stored in matter. Coal is black and cold, but it stores light and heat from the sunlight of over three hundred million years ago.

Drowned in swamps and shifting oceans, crushed under huge layers of rock, the leaves and stems of the plants turned hard and black, but they did not change back to the original chemicals.

When you burn coal, the fossils of plants turn back to chemicals, something like the ones from which they were made, and the ancient sunlight is released — as fire.

Prehistoric ferns grew in large numbers, using the sunlight to build up plant fibers from the simple chemicals of the air and water.

sands of times a second in a loudspeaker. Work may be changing the temperature of something.

We measure energy by the amount of work it does. We measure it in *foot-pounds*. For example, 20 foot-pounds is the amount of energy it would take to lift 2 pounds 10 feet, or 10 pounds 2 feet, or 5 pounds 4 feet. We also measure energy in *calories*. A "small calorie," the kind people count when they are dieting, is a thousand times bigger — so a man on a strict diet might eat only enough food to give him 3,000,000 foot-pounds of energy a day. We also measure energy in *joules, ergs, horsepower-hours, kilowatt-hours,* and all sorts of units, depending on the kind of work we mean.

How do we measure energy?

In the year 1900, every physicist in the world would have told you that we cannot make new energy — we can only use energy which exists already. Of course we can make electrical

Can we "make" energy?

energy, but we make it out of other energy, energy in another form.

Energy exists in many forms, and we have learned how to change it from form to form. Suppose you build a fire. It gives you *heat-energy*. With that you could boil water and use the steam to push the piston of the steam engine, which would turn a wheel, giving you *mechanical energy*. That might in turn drive a dynamo, changing the mechanical energy into *electrical energy*. That electricity could work a lamp, which would turn it into *light-energy*. Or a stove, which would change it back to heat-energy. Or a motor, which would change it back to mechanical energy.

In doing all this, said the scientists of 1900, you have not added any energy to the universe. You took some energy which had been stored up in matter — just as mechanical energy is stored in a wound-up watchspring — and *converted* that energy until it had done the work you wanted.

They were nearly right, which in science, where there is no "nearly," means that they were wrong.

Energy can be changed to other forms. Fire (heat energy) boils water. Steam drives an engine which turns a wheel (mechanical energy), which drives a dynamo (electrical energy), which lights a lamp (light energy).

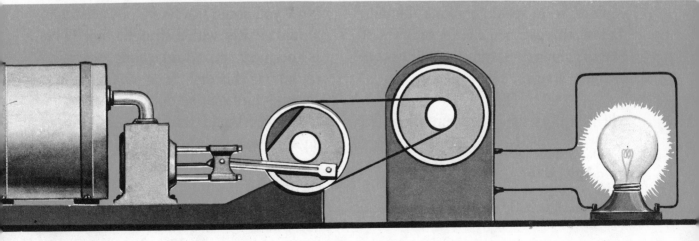

The scientists of 1900 were also sure we could never destroy any energy. We could only lose it.

Energy is always leaking away and tak-

Do we burn up energy? ing forms in which we cannot catch it and use it. The fire under your boiler heats other things besides the wa-

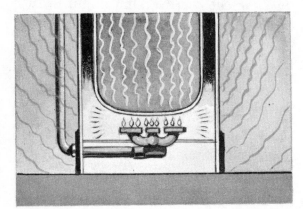

Fire under a boiler heats other things besides water.

ter in the boiler. The steam seeps out around the piston. The air around the hot cylinder of the steam engine warms up and blows away. The dynamo heats up from friction, and this energy is also carried away by the air. Your electric wires get warm. The light bulb gives off heat as well as light, and that, too, is carried away. So as you go on converting energy from one form to another, you are, so to speak, cooking the wind. At last, this escaped energy radiates off, like the sun's rays, into the endless cold of outer space.

But it still exists somewhere out there.

Where does used energy go to? It is not destroyed. The human race sends about 90,-000,000,000,000,000,000 foot-pounds

of energy out into space each year. So in 1900, physicists had the idea that we can never change the amount of energy in the universe, and they were so sure of this that they called it a scientific law — the *Law of the Conservation of Energy*. Now we know it is only half a law.

Suppose you were to hold a lighted

What happens when we burn matter? match to the corner of a stack of pa-per. The paper would catch fire and the bright hot flames would eat across the sheets until the paper was burned up Some heat-energy and some light-energy would be given off, while one half an ounce of solid matter would seem to vanish. A bit of fluffy ash and a floating cloud of smoke would apparently be all that was left.

Wouldn't you have changed that mat-ter into energy then? Doesn't that mean matter and energy are really forms of the same thing after all?

In 1900, you could not have found a

Can we change matter into energy? single physicist who would have an-swered "yes" to those questions. Now you could not find a physicist who would answer with a straight "no." This is the most important change of mind in human history. It is changing our lives — and maybe our deaths.

So we should think carefully about such an experiment with a stack of pa-per. To burn it scientifically you would have to burn it inside a can. You would have to use a big can, so as to hold all

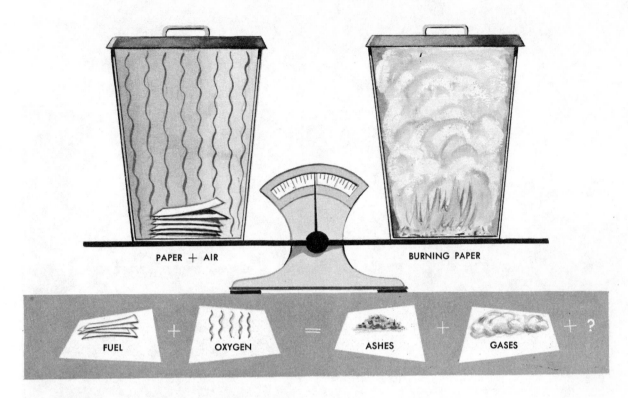

PAPER + AIR   BURNING PAPER

FUEL + OXYGEN = ASHES + GASES + ?

the air you needed for the fire. You would have to seal it up tight, so that absolutely no matter could get in or out. You would have to place the can on a scale while the paper burned and the can cooled off. And your scale would not show any change in weight.

In 1900, we all would have agreed that the ash and smoke and gases from the flame weighed *exactly* what the paper and air weighed to begin with. For we all thought then that there was another law of nature, called the *Law of the Conservation of Mass,* which said that no matter is ever added to the universe or taken away from it. Well, we know now that there actually *would* be a tiny loss of weight in that can. You could not have converted one half an ounce of matter into energy. But you would have converted one ten-billionth of an ounce of matter into energy. No scale in the world is good enough to

show it. But you would have done it. How do we know?

In the year 1905, a young German-born scientist was

When did physicists change their mind?

working in the Swiss Patent Office, checking other people's inventions. And he wrote a paper about what he called his *Theory of Relativity.* He hoped it would explain some facts about light and about the stars which had been mystifying physicists and astronomers for years. It did. It did something else, too. In this paper, Albert Einstein, one of the great scientific minds of all time, wrote a sentence which has become the most famous sentence of the twentieth century. Einstein did not write his sentence in words. He wrote it in algebra, the language of mathematics that uses letters of the alphabet to stand for numbers: $E = mc^2$.

ENERGY

AMOUNT OF MATTER

VELOCITY OF LIGHT

$$E = MC^2$$

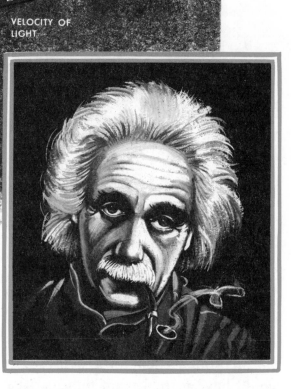

ALBERT EINSTEIN

We read this statement as "E equals m times c squared." It says that if you take a certain amount of matter and convert it into energy, you can calculate the number of foot-pounds you will get (which we have written down as E, for energy) by multiplying the number of pounds of matter you wipe out (which we have written down as m, for mass) by a certain number that is always the same (which we have written as c^2). Or, if you change energy into matter, the same formula will tell you how much mass you get in exchange for your energy.

What does $E = mc^2$ mean?

Einstein did not just say that this is what *would* happen if it *could* happen. He said it *does* happen. All the physicists had known that energy can be stored in matter and gotten out again, but they believed that this did not change the amount of matter. Einstein's brilliant theory said that when energy is stored in matter, it takes the form of a little additional mass, and when the energy is released, the mass goes back to what it was. In other words, instead of a Law of the Conservation of Energy and a separate Law of the Conservation of Mass, we now had one law, the *Law of Conservation of Mass-and-Energy.*

And this suggested a very strange idea. It was not some particular little bits of energy or mass that might change back and forth. If only we know how, we could change *any* mass into energy.

Does $E = mc^2$ work for all kinds of matter?

No one did much about it for many years. In the first place, no one knew where to start. In the second place, scientists felt happy enough just having a tidy new theory which helped them calculate things they could not measure with instruments and which explained various odd facts they had never understood before. Most of them paid no attention to one letter in the famous equation. That was the letter c.

Now, in Einstein's theory, c stands for speed of light. **How much energy can we get from matter?** Light travels at 186,000 miles per second. The expression c^2 ("c squared") means the speed of light *multiplied by itself*. It gives us a gigantic number, 34,596,-000,000. If we do the arithmetic using this number, we find that from very little mass we get an astonishing amount of energy. When we burn a pound of coal in the ordinary way, we might get 10 million foot-pounds of energy. This is good. But if we could convert the whole pound of mass into energy, then by Einstein's formula we would get 30 million billion foot-pounds of energy. This is better.

If we only knew how ...

Inside the Atom

The ancient Greek philosophers wondered what would happen **What is matter made of?** if we took some solid matter — like stone or metal — and kept grinding it up into finer and finer powder. Some said that no matter how tiny the particles became, it would always be possible to break them up into still smaller particles by grinding harder. They believed that matter was made of a stuff called *hyle* (which is Greek for "stuff"), and that this was smooth right through and could be divided up endlessly.

Others said that no matter how hard or long we ground, we could not get the particles smaller than a certain size. They believed matter was made of separate hard lumps called *atoms* (which is Greek for "can't be cut"), and that these were the smallest things or particles there were.

Some ancient Greeks said matter could be ground endlessly. Others said atoms were the smallest things.

21

The second group was nearer to the truth, of course. Matter usually does consist of atoms. But they were wrong in thinking there was nothing smaller than an atom. And they certainly picked the wrong name for their fundamental particle. The atom can be cut.

For 2,200 years, no one had anything new or important to say on the subject. Then in **What are elements?** 1803, an English schoolteacher named John Dalton began to study atoms seriously. He figured out that some things are made up of only one kind of atom. These are pure *elements*. Gold and mercury and oxygen are elements. Other things are made of two, three or even more different kinds of atoms. These are *mixtures* and *compounds*. In mixtures the different elements are simply jumbled together. Air is a mixture of oxygen and nitrogen and other gases. In compounds, atoms of different kinds are actually linked together in little groups. Water is a compound in which each oxygen atom is linked up with two hydrogen atoms in a tiny package called a water *molecule*.

Dalton weighed and measured elements and compounds until **What did Dalton discover about atoms?** he began to find some rules for the ways in which the atoms could be linked and separated. He was able to calculate how much different atoms weighed compared to each other. But he still thought that atoms were little pellets—too small to see and too tough to cut, but not really different from grains of dust.

An atom — even an atom of iron in the **Are atoms solid?** steel armor-plate of a warship, or an atom of carbon in a diamond — is mostly empty space. The big old solid world around us is not solid at all. It is made of tiny spots of matter hanging or whirling quite far apart in open space.

Then why, if you pound your fist on the table, doesn't your hand go *into* the table-top? Because your hand, too, is empty space, and because strong electrical forces between the whirling spots hold them away from each other. Those forces, jostling the atoms in your flesh, are what you feel as the bang of your hand on the table.

We are sure of this although no one has ever actually seen an atom. Atoms are too small to see — 100 million of them in a row would take up less than an inch.

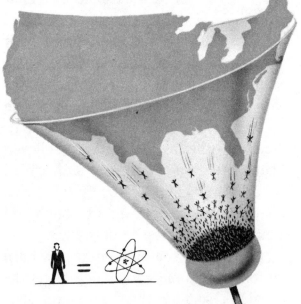

If people were no larger than an atom, the entire population of the U. S. could sit on the head of a pin, and there would still be space for several millions more.

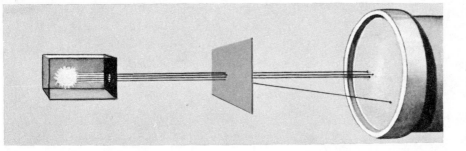

Most of the atomic bullets go through the "solid" metal — this shows that atoms are mostly empty space.

In 1911, an English physicist named Ernest Rutherford invented a way of testing whether atoms are solid. He shot them with even smaller particles. He got his "bullets" out of atoms of the element *radium,* which Pierre and Marie Curie of France had discovered and extracted from certain rocks. Radium atoms have a strange property. They are always breaking up little by little and flinging out tiny fragments of matter and little streams of energy. Several elements do this. They are called *radioactive* elements.

Can we see atoms?

Rutherford put some radium in a sort of gun-barrel made of lead. He aimed it at a target made of a fluorescent screen, like the front of a television picture tube. In between, he put a thin sheet of pure gold — but thin as it was, it was thousands of atoms thick, and shooting at it with the atomic "bullets" was like shooting with real bullets at armor-plate fifty feet thick. Yet the atomic bullets went through, and made little sparkles on the target screen.

How did we learn what is inside the atom?

And some of the sparkles were way off to the side, as if the atomic bullets had ricocheted. Rutherford realized what had happened. The bullets got

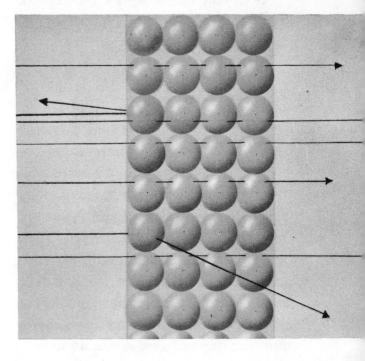

But some of the atomic bullets bounce back or to the side — this shows that inside the atom there is a hard kernel or a "nucleus."

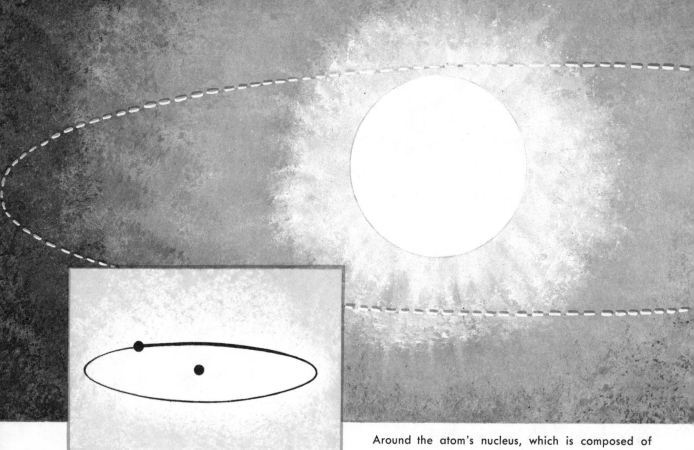

Around the atom's nucleus, which is composed of protons and neutrons, spin particles called electrons.

through easily because the gold atoms were not solid stuff, but open space. And in the middle of each atom there was a lump of mass, off which a bullet sometimes bounced. Rutherford decided to call this lump the *nucleus* of the atom, from the Latin name for the pit in a piece of fruit.

How do we look at atoms? Now we have hundreds of different devices for studying atoms, ranging from regular X-ray machines to fantastic jungles of wires and magnets and vacuum tubes called by such names as *cyclotron* and *bevatron*. One great *synchrotron* near New York City uses four thousand tons of magnets and a huge doughnut of metal a half mile around. With these huge machines, we can glimpse a little of what is going on in the tiny universe of the atom.

What is inside the atom? Scientists have put together all the facts they have gathered about the atom and they have a kind of picture of it in their minds. It looks something like a picture of our solar system. In the middle of the solar system the huge sun hangs in empty space. Around it, one inside the other, in paths or "orbits" like circles pulled out of shape, spin the planets, like our earth and Mars and Saturn.

In the middle of an atom, hanging in empty space, is the nucleus. Around it, in orbits like circles pulled out of shape, spin other tiny particles.

How big is the nucleus? The nucleus is so small it is hard even to think about how small it is. The atom itself is small—there are 6,000,000,000,000,000,000,000 atoms

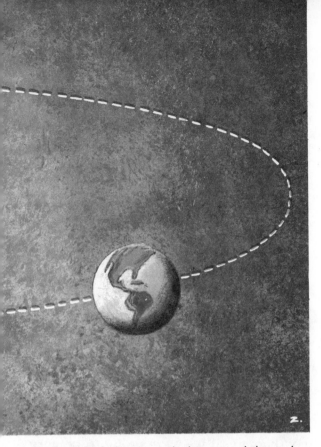

The action of electrons spinning around the nucleus is much like the orbit of the earth around the sun.

in a drop of water. If you had that many strawberries, you could cover the whole world with a layer of strawberries seventy-five feet thick. And the nucleus takes up only $\frac{1}{1,000,000,000,000}$ of the space of the atom. If the nucleus were the size of a strawberry and you put it down in the middle of a big football field, right on the fifty-yard line, the outer "planets" of the atom would be going around in orbits way out over the spectators' heads, or even behind them.

But even though the nucleus takes up only a trillionth of the space in an atom, it has almost all the mass of the atom. Thus it is tremendously heavy for its size. A nucleus the size of a strawberry would weigh about 75 million tons. If you did put it down in the middle of a football field, the earth could not hold it. It would simply crush its way through

sand and rock, down and down to the core of the world.

The nucleus is mostly made of two kinds of particles, *protons* and *neutrons*. The outer planet-particles are *electrons*. There are two kinds of electricity, which we call *positive* and *negative*. Two things that have positive electric charges push each other away. So do two things with negative charges. But if a positively charged thing and a negatively charged thing are near together, they pull at each other very strongly.

What is the nucleus made of?

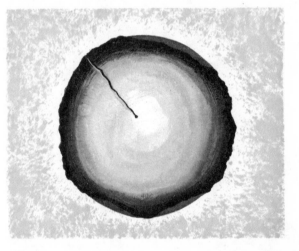

A nucleus that was the size of a strawberry would smash the earth's crust by its enormous weight.

The proton has a positive electric charge of a certain strength. The neutron has no electric charge at all. The electron, which is about 1,800 times lighter than the other two particles, has a negative electric charge — just as

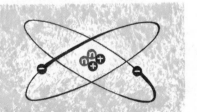

HELIUM ATOM

25

strong as the proton's, but the opposite kind. The nucleus or "sun" of the atom, therefore, has a positive charge. The outer electrons or "planets" have a negative charge. And the whole atom itself usually has no charge, because there are just as many protons in the nucleus as electrons whirling around it, so the charges balance or cancel each other. In the ordinary sodium atom, which is one of the atoms in salt, there are eleven protons and twelve neutrons in the nucleus, and eleven electrons going around in orbit.

By now, you will have thought of two questions. One is easy and one is hard.

The pull of the nucleus keeps the electrons in orbit just as the string keeps the bucket in its orbit.

If things witn opposite charges attract each other, why doesn't the positive nucleus pull the negative electrons right down into it and just collapse the atom? Easy. The speed of

Why do the electrons keep flying around the nucleus?

the electrons makes them keep trying to fly off, away from the nucleus. Tie a weight to a string and whirl it around fast. You can feel the pull of the weight trying to fly away from your hand at the center. You have to pull a little to keep the weight in orbit. The electrical pull of the nucleus keeps the electrons in their paths, just as the pull of the sun's gravity keeps the earth in its orbit.

And if things with the same charges push each other away, why don't the protons in the nucleus just go flying off from each other in all directions? That one is hard. That is where atomic energy comes in.

By the way, if we were going to be very careful about words, most energy really could be called *atomic energy*. Because, as Einstein showed us, when energy flows around the universe it is always changing the mass of atoms. But when we think about the insides of the atom, we can see that there are two sorts of energy. One has to do with the outer electrons. The other has to do with the nucleus.

Is atomic energy a special kind of energy?

When two different atoms are linked together in a chemical compound, the nucleus of one does not join the nucleus of the other. Instead, some of the outer electrons change their orbits. Sometimes the two nuclei will share a few of these electrons. When a carbon atom forms the gas called methane, for instance, it shares electrons with four hydrogen

How do atoms form chemicals?

atoms. Or sometimes one nucleus steals an electron from the other by a complicated magnetic trick, and this leaves the thief-atom negatively charged and the victim-atom positively charged, so they stick together. This is how sodium and chlorine combine to make ordinary salt. It is as if the poor sodium atom kept following the chlorine atom around in the hope of getting its electron back. This kind of linking is called a *chemical bond*.

What is chemical energy? Sometimes when you make or break a chemical link, energy is given out, and this is called *chemical energy*. When an atom of carbon in a chunk of coal links up with two atoms of oxygen from the air, a compound called carbon dioxide — a gas with no color or smell — is formed, and at the same time heat-energy and light-energy are released. In other words, you have a fire. But this does not disturb the carbon nucleus or the oxygen nuclei.

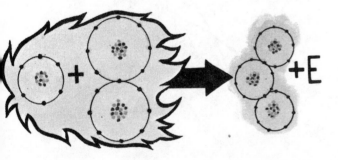

Heat given off when a carbon atom joins with two oxygen atoms is a simple form of chemical energy.

If you actually change the nucleus of an atom in order to get energy, you are doing something quite different. We ought to call this *nuclear energy,* but we usually just call it *atomic energy.*

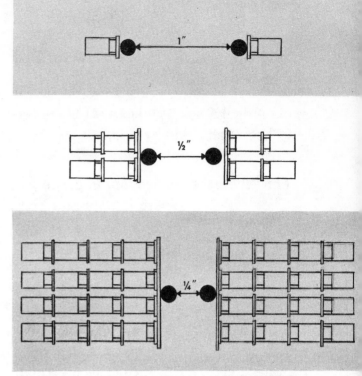

Things with the same electric charge push each other apart. When you divide the *distance* between them by 2, you multiply the *push* between them by 2 x 2.

Where does "atomic energy" come from? We wish to turn matter into energy. Well, then, we have to look at the place where practically all the mass in the universe is — the nucleus of the atom. We do not know much about the nucleus yet. One of the questions scientists are still wondering about is that hard question of yours: What holds it together?

Something must. We know how strong the forces are that push apart things that have the same electric charge. The closer together the two things are, the more powerful is the force that pushes them away from each other. If there is a certain push between them when they are 1 inch apart, there will be 4 times as much push when they are ½ inch apart, and 16 times at ¼ inch, and 64 times at ⅛ inch, and 256 as strong at ¹⁄₁₆ inch. At that rate, you can imagine how

27

hard the push is between two protons rammed into a nucleus $\frac{1}{2,000,000,000,000}$ of an inch apart. It takes a lot of energy to keep them side by side.

This energy is called *binding energy*.

What holds the nucleus together? There is only one kind of atom that does not need any binding energy. That is the atom of hydrogen gas, which only has one proton in its nucleus. Some of the heavier kinds of atoms, with dozens of protons in their nuclei, have to have enormous amounts of binding energy. Where do they get it?

From mass. No one knows how a nucleus converts some of its own mass into energy in order to pull itself together. But physicists all agree that this is what happens. They can prove this by very carefully measuring the mass of an atom. Except for hydrogen, every atom weighs just a little bit less than it *ought* to.

Take helium gas, for instance. The helium nucleus

How much binding energy is in the nucleus? helium nucleus contains two protons and two neutrons. A proton by itself weighs 1.00758 of the tiny "mass units" that scientists have in-

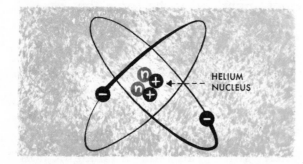

HELIUM NUCLEUS

vented for these measurements. A neutron weighs 1.00894. So the whole helium nucleus ought to weigh 4.03304. Instead, it weighs 4.00279. More than $\frac{3}{100}$ of a "mass unit" are missing. Using Einstein's $E = mc^2$ formula, we can calculate how much energy this is — what the scientists call 28 million "electron volts." This is only a tiny fraction of a foot-pound. But it is what keeps the universe from going *whoosh!* and turning into hydrogen. And it is what lets us turn matter into atomic energy.

There are hundreds of different kinds of atoms in the uni-

How many kinds of atoms are there? atoms in the universe. One way of sorting them out is to find out how many protons they have in the nucleus. All the atoms with one proton are *hydrogen* atoms. All with two are called *helium*. All with three, *lithium*. Four,

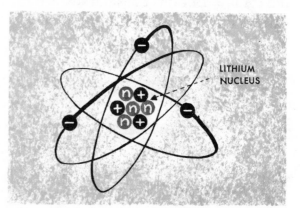

LITHIUM NUCLEUS

beryllium. Five, *boron*. Six, *carbon*. Seven, *nitrogen*. Eight, *oxygen*. And so on up to ninety-two, which is *uranium*. That is the heaviest kind of atom found in nature, though we have made a few heavier ones with our cyclotrons and atomic furnaces.

Each kind of atom with a certain number of protons is a different *element*. Until recently, we thought we were saying all we had to say about any atom if we just told what element it was. This, of course, is not so hard to do, because the number of protons in the nucleus is the same as the number of electrons out in orbit. These electrons are what make the atoms link chemically with other kinds of atoms or refuse to link with them. So clever chemists can always separate different elements.

But there is another kind of particle in the nucleus — the neutron. Atoms with the same number of protons may come in different varieties, with different numbers of neutrons. Even the lightest and simplest element, hydrogen, comes in three varieties. The usual kind has one proton and no neutrons. Another, quite rare, has a proton and a neutron. It is sometimes called *deuterium,* but it is just "heavy" hydrogen. A third kind, called *tritium,* has to be made artificially. It has one proton and two neutrons, but it is still called hydrogen.

Are all the atoms of an element the same?

Each of these varieties is called an *isotope*. The name was taken from the Greek words meaning "the same place," because isotopes of the same element always appear together in the chemists' lists. And that is more important than it sounds. Since different isotopes of the same element have the same number of outer electrons, they are just the same in chemical linkings and unlinkings, so that chemists have had a difficult time separating them. And since different isotopes of the same element behave quite differently when it comes to converting mass and releasing nuclear energy, they *must* be separated.

We have some wonderful machines that actually sort out atoms by weight. But they can only do it with a few atoms at a time.

What is an isotope?

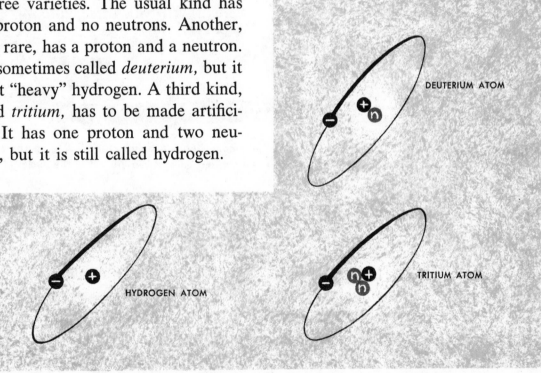

DEUTERIUM ATOM

HYDROGEN ATOM

TRITIUM ATOM

The usual hydrogen atom has 1 proton; deuterium has 1 proton, 1 neutron; tritium has 1 proton, 2 neutrons.

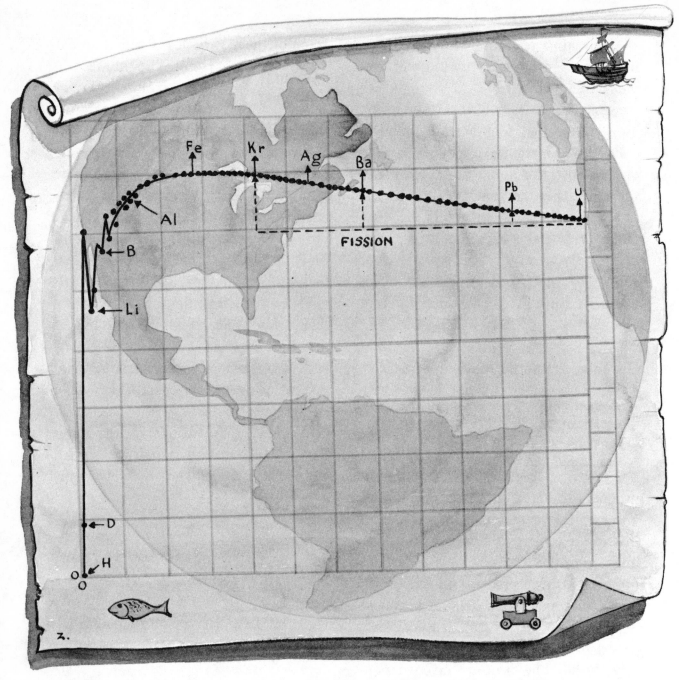

If you dig for buried treasure, the best thing you could possibly have is a map. The binding energy curve, a chart of all the isotopes in the world, tells us where we can dig energy treasure out of the nuclei of atoms.

What is the "binding energy curve"?

This, however, is enough to give us the facts we need to make a great chart of isotopes called the *binding energy curve*. This chart tells us how much mass is "missing" from the nucleus of each of the hundreds of isotopes we have found or made. In other words, it tells us how much matter each kind of nucleus has mysteriously converted into energy to keep itself together.

This chart is why all the physicists were so excited when word spread that Hahn had turned the metal uranium into the metal barium. For the chart is like a map of buried treasure. It tells us where to dig for atomic energy.

30

It tells us that ordinary hydrogen has no mass missing. It tells us that helium, the next heavier element, has quite a lot missing. As we go up through heavier and heavier kinds of atoms, we find more and more mass missing *for each particle in the nucleus* — up to a point. Up to a point — the element iron — and then, strangely enough, we find less and less mass missing for each particle in the heavier and heavier isotopes.

Did the big atoms have the most binding energy?

When we get to the heaviest element — the three isotopes of uranium — and look up how much mass is missing from the 234, or 235, or 238 nuclear particles — we find that much less of it has been turned into energy than in such middleweight elements as barium.

Think for a moment what this means.

It means that if we split up a uranium atom into two pieces, we will get two smaller atoms — and something else. There are 92 protons in the uranium nucleus. Let us say the two pieces

How can we get at some binding energy?

happen to be not quite equal. One might have 36 protons in it — that would be the gas krypton. The other would have the remaining 56 protons — it would be barium. When you look at the chart you see that barium and krypton have *more mass missing* from them than uranium. So suddenly, some mass has disappeared from the universe.

And Einstein's formula tells us what has become of it. It has turned into energy — into the tremendous force with which the fragments of the uranium fly apart.

Maybe it is a little hard to see why this is energy we could use. Why doesn't this mass turn into energy that the nucleus uses inside of itself? As a matter of fact, it was hard for some physicists to be sure about this for a while. One answer is that binding energy does not work by brute force. It is something like the law that says you can't leave the country if you owe money to the government. The binding energy was energy that was given off when the protons and neutrons

Why doesn't binding energy stay inside the atom?

Protons and neutrons owe energy to the nucleus and they are supposed to stay there until the debt is paid.

were packed together, and ordinarily they cannot get away unless this energy, this missing mass, is restored to the nucleus. But even if you can't leave legally, you could always *break* out. That is what happens when we split the atom.

And that is why the chart means this also: If we could mash a couple of hydrogen nuclei together so as to form a helium nucleus, we would also wipe out some matter. We would wipe out more matter, in fact, than by splitting uranium. The energy would be prodigious. It would be like making a sun. For this *is* how the sun gets its energy.

Atom Smashing

Who discovered radioactivity?

In 1896, before we knew anything about $E = mc^2$ or what the atom is like, a French physicist named Henri Becquerel had a slight accident in his laboratory. He was testing some uranium compounds for something and discovered that they gave off energy all by themselves. Soon after that Pierre and Marie Curie began to discover a whole group of new elements that did the same thing. Madame Curie named this strange behavior *radioactivity*.

For a long time, nobody was sure how radioactivity worked. Many experiments were done to find out just what these mysterious "rays" were. Some of them at last turned out to be helium atoms with their electrons knocked off. Some turned out to be fast-moving electrons. Some turned out to be real rays like very powerful X-rays. But what were they doing in those atoms? And why did they come out?

Do atoms ever split by themselves?

It slowly dawned on the scientists that what they were looking at were *atoms breaking down*. This was a rather frightening idea, for two reasons. In the first place, everyone at that time still thought atoms were unbreakable, everlasting little pellets. This showed they were not. And if pieces broke off an atom, what was left must be a different atom. That meant elements were changing into other elements. And if elements changed into other elements when particles flew out, then atoms probably were not the particles that "could not be cut" (as their name said), but were bundles of still smaller particles.

Why was radioactivity important?

In the second place, the particles flew out with great energy and the rays were very energetic, too. These atoms seemed to be *making* energy, which everybody in

The French physicist, Antoine Henri Becquerel (1852-1908), discovered natural radioactivity, the invisible radiation of uranium. With Pierre and Marie Curie, he won the Nobel Prize in physics for his great discovery.

The strange rays from uranium blackened a photographic film right through a light-proof cover, Becquerel found.

Pierre Curie of France (1859-1906) and his wife Marie (1867-1934) were the discoverers of radium in 1898. In addition to sharing the Nobel Prize with Becquerel and her husband in 1903, Marie Curie received the Nobel award again in 1911, in chemistry.

Let's pretend that you were very rich and that you had the very large sum of one million dollars, even after taxes.

And now let us also suppose that you have promised to give away half of all your money on every Friday of the week — even on Friday the thirteenth.

Then on the first Friday, you will give away $500,000. On the second Friday, you will give away $250,000 more. On the third Friday, $125,000 more.

Then we say that the "half-life" of your money is one week, because in one week, one half disappears.

But no matter how much you give, you will never go altogether broke.

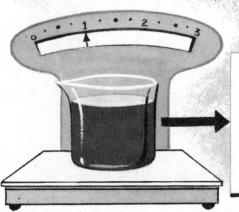

U-238 = 4,500,000,000 YEARS

RADIUM = 1,620 YEARS

FRANCIUM = 21 MINUTES

THORIUM = 14,000,000,000 YEARS

POLONIUM = 138 DAYS

NEPTUNIUM = 2⅓ DAYS

And — every radioactive isotope has its own "half-life."

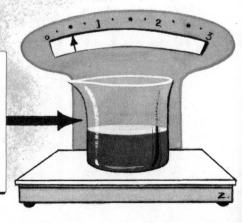

those days *knew* was all wrong. When Einstein came along and said that this energy was converted from mass, it seemed like the best explanation.

So a lot of what we now know about atoms came from that laboratory accident.

Now all those radioactive atoms were quite heavy. It seemed that a heavy nucleus was not too sturdy. This suggested that if we could only smash up heavy atoms, instead of letting them decay slowly by themselves, we might change one element into another and perhaps even release energy much faster. But we had nothing with which to smash them.

The neutron is a quiet little particle.

Why are neutrons good atomic bullets? There are probably more neutrons in the universe than anything else, but it was not till 1930 that we found them — hiding right in the middle of everything. For years, physicists had been trying to make a picture of the atom that would explain the things atoms did. They tried all sorts of wild combinations of the positive proton and the negative electron. Then an Englishman named James Chadwick suggested, "Why not try drawing it with a particle a little bit bigger than the proton but without any electric charge?" Everyone realized this was the answer. And they realized that here, also, was the thing with which to smash heavy nuclei.

The problem is to hit the nucleus. Suppose you shoot at it with a positively charged proton. As it passes the negatively charged electrons, they will pull it to one side. As it approaches the posi-

tively charged nucleus, that will push it away. Suppose you shoot an electron. The positive nucleus will certainly pull the negative electron toward it. But electrons are too light. They cannot do enough damage. The neutron is heavy and it will not be pulled off its course.

So physicists set up various machines **How do we split uranium atoms?** for using other particles to bounce neutrons out of the nuclei of light metals like beryllium. And they started shooting.

They kept shooting for seven years. All sorts of things happened. They made new elements, heavier than uranium. They made old elements radioactive.

And one day in January 1939, Otto Hahn found a little barium in the uranium that he had been bombarding with neutrons. The news spread that the uranium nucleus had been split, and young Dr. Dunning, remembering the binding energy chart, rushed up to his laboratory to measure the release of nuclear energy.

When a neutron hits a uranium nucleus, **What happens when a uranium atom splits?** one of three things can happen. (1) It may bounce. That's that. (2) It may just stay there. Nothing would happen till later. So we will think about this. (3) It may break the nucleus apart.

Suppose a neutron hits a nucleus of one of the three ordinary isotopes of uranium. This is the isotope with 92 protons and 143 neutrons in it — called

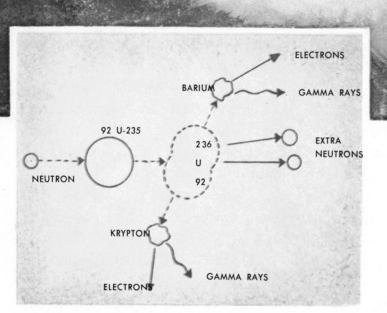

ELECTRONS

BARIUM

GAMMA RAYS

92 U-235

2 36

U

92

EXTRA
NEUTRONS

NEUTRON

KRYPTON

GAMMA RAYS

ELECTRONS

Z.

When a neutron bullet breaks a nucleus in two, this splitting is known as fission. The two pieces fly off with enormous energy and become new, smaller nuclei. Two new neutron bullets also shoot out.

U-235. The new neutron makes it U-236. But for some reason, U-236 never stays together. It bursts into pieces. There are many ways it can break. Suppose this time the biggest piece is a barium nucleus, with 56 protons and 88 neutrons. Another piece is krypton, with 36 protons and 54 neutrons. And there are at least two extra neutrons by themselves. *They* are *very* important. And there is a lot of energy, which makes all the pieces shoot off at terrific speeds.

This is called *fission*.

It is very nice to be able to smash atoms.

What is a "chain reaction"?

But it is not a useful thing to do unless you get more energy out of it than you put into it. If you have to keep a building full of equipment pumping neutrons into uranium to split a few nuclei, you are just playing.

Think back for a moment to the paper-burning experiment. You touch a lighted match to the corner of one sheet. The paper catches fire. The flames spread. You do not have to set each

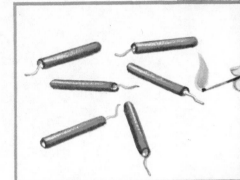

If firecrackers are separate, you must set them off one at a time. But if they are attached together, you only have to light one, and each will then set off the next one.

part of the paper on fire separately. You just heat up one small bit of it until that bursts into flame. The heat from that flame starts the next few fibers burning, and they light the next bit, and so on. This is called a *chain reaction*.

That is what we want to do with uranium. We need a chain reaction in which each bursting nucleus will shoot out neutrons that break up other nuclei near it. The two loose neutrons that fly out in the fission of a uranium nucleus give us atomic energy we can use.

What do we need to make a chain reaction?
But now suppose — as we again think of the experiment with the match and the paper — that the paper is damp. Each bit of paper would need so much heat to get it lit that the sections next to it would have burned away before it got started. The fire would go out.

A chain reaction is something like the firecrackers that are attached to each other. When a uranium atom splits, it shoots out neutron bullets that split nearby atoms, which split other atoms, and so forth.

In the same way, we need the right isotope of uranium for our atomic chain reaction. It has to have a nucleus that splits easily and that shoots out loose neutrons. The U-235 isotope is excel-

37

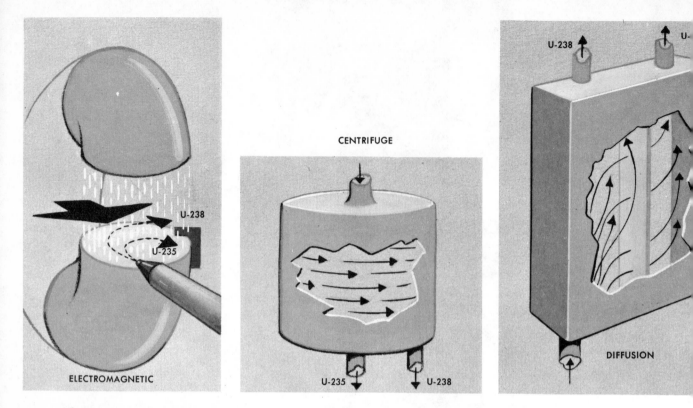

CENTRIFUGE

U-238

U-235

ELECTROMAGNETIC

U-235   U-238

U-238   U-

DIFFUSION

Scientists have figured out three ways to separate U-235 from U-238. In the electromagnetic way, the uranium is shot between the poles of a magnet, which separates the heavier atoms from the lighter ones. In the centrifuge way, the uranium is whirled around and the heavy atoms swing to the outside. In the diffusion way, more light atoms seep through the divider than heavy ones. Separation is necessary to make atomic fuel.

lent. But U-235 is hard to come by. No matter where natural uranium comes from — the Congo or Canada or Russia or in meteorites from outer space — it always contains the same amounts of its three isotopes. And less than a hundredth of it is U-235.

Another uranium isotope, U-234, only shows up in faint traces. We can hardly tell it is there. More than 99 per cent of uranium is the heavy isotope, U-238, with 92 protons and 146 neutrons. Unfortunately, it is like damp paper. The neutrons crash into the U-238 nucleus — and stay there. This is not bad. It has its uses. But it will not keep the atomic fire going.

Will other elements or isotopes work?

What isotopes are good atomic fuel?

Yes — a man-made element called *plutonium* is excellent atomic fuel. Plutonium has 94 protons and 145 neutrons. We make it by putting U-238 in an atomic oven and "cooking" it in neutrons, so to speak. When a neutron hits the U-238 nucleus and stays there, it gives us a new uranium isotope with 92 protons and 147 neutrons. That is just too many neutrons, and this is a very shaky nucleus. But it does not break up. Instead it soon begins to break down. One of the neutrons mysteriously turns into a proton, and an electron — of all things — suddenly shoots out of the nucleus. Now we have a new element called *neptunium,* with 93 protons and 146 neutrons. But this nucleus is still rather rickety. Again a neutron changes into a proton and an electron pops out. Now we have plutonium.

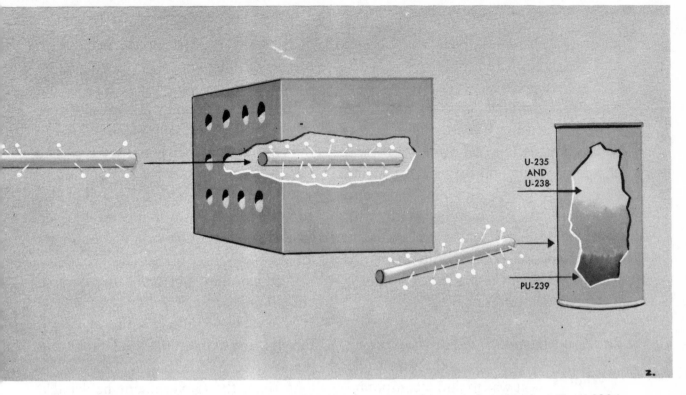

Scientists have found a way to change uranium-238 into the more useful atomic fuel plutonium. The U-238 is put into a reactor where it is bombarded with neutrons from U-235. Many of the U-238 atoms are built up into plutonium-239 atoms, which can be separated chemically. At one time, scientists thought that plutonium was an artificial element, but we now know that it occurs naturally and is found in the mineral pitchblende.

But in order to have it, we first have to

Can we make atomic fuel?

have a good atomic oven with plenty of neutrons. In other words, a chain reaction. In other words, U-235. That was the problem that nagged at American scientists in the years between 1939 and 1942.

Professor Fermi was sure he could build an atomic furnace that would work — and which could be used as an oven to cook up plutonium. Other scientists had calculated that if only they could get enough plutonium or enough U-235, they could make a bomb that would knock America's enemies right out of the war.

For during these years, Hitler's armies beat down nation after nation in Europe, and the Japanese struck without warning at Pearl Harbor and con-

quered hundreds of islands in the Pacific. Our scientists were afraid that the German scientists would make an atom bomb for Hitler, and that this cruel madman would rule the world.

Working day and night, chemists and physicists tried to invent a way of separating enough U-235 to start an atomic furnace.

One group said the way to do it was the

How do we separate isotopes?

way it was done in a mass spectrometer, by shooting electrically charged streams of uranium atoms between the poles of magnets. The government spent millions and millions of dollars to build *electromagnetic separators* at an out-of-the-way place in Tennessee called Oak Ridge. It was, and is, a good factory for

39

separating isotopes, but it could not make enough U-235.

Another group said the way to do it was by *centrifugal force* — the force that makes things try to fly outward when they are whirled around in a circle. If we could make a gas or steam with uranium in it, and whirl it around in a tank, the compounds made with heaviest uranium atoms would go to the outside and we could pump them off. The Government had a factory built to try this, but it did not work well.

Professor Dunning and his Columbia group said the way to do it was to find a compound of uranium that was a gas, and put it in a tank with a porous wall — a wall with thousands and thousands of tiny holes in it — holes so small it would be hard for the gas to leak through. The particles of compound would be banging around

What is gaseous diffusion?

in the tank, and the ones made with heavier atoms would be moving more slowly than the lighter ones. So it would be the fast, light ones that would have the better chance of pushing through the porous wall — where they could be collected on the other side. Of course, some of the heavier particles would also get through, so we would have to do the filtering over and over again in tank after tank.

The gas that had to be used was a compound called *uranium hexafluoride*. It is a vicious stuff. It would eat right through ordinary tanks and pipes and pumps like a horrible acid. So for a long time, the Government held back. Then it told Professor Dunning to go ahead and design a huge factory to be built out of special materials at Oak Ridge. More millions of dollars were spent—and the *gaseous diffusion plant*, known in wartime code as K-25, worked.

(1) Mining it. (2) Milling it. (3) Refining it. (4) Separating U-235 from U-238 in a gaseous diffusion plant.

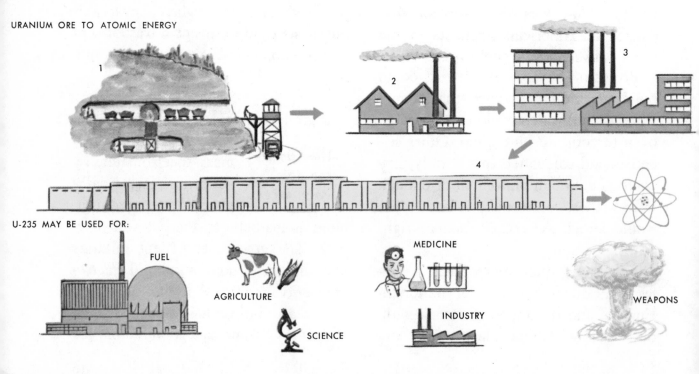

URANIUM ORE TO ATOMIC ENERGY

U-235 MAY BE USED FOR:

FUEL

AGRICULTURE

SCIENCE

MEDICINE

INDUSTRY

WEAPONS

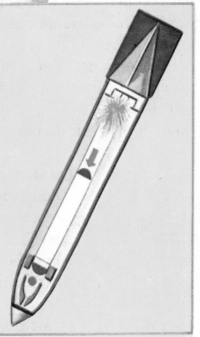

At Bikini atoll in the Pacific, the U.S. set off an atom bomb under water. The cross section shows how an A-bomb works.

It is still working. It is an extraordinary place. Miles and miles of empty corridors lined with panels of dials and signal lights — miles and miles of tank rooms and pump rooms with no man to be seen — hundreds of miles of wires and automatic machinery — and every once in a while, a man will come down the hallway on a bicycle, copy a number from a dial, and ride back to the main control room. This is the place where America's atomic energy starts.

What does an isotope separation-plant look like?

Once you have enough of the right isotope, there is no trick at all to starting a chain reaction. You simply put enough of the isotope together in a lump and — off it goes!

How do we start the chain reaction?

How much is enough? It depends on the isotope. It depends on whether you are making a bomb or a furnace. It depends on how fast you let the neutrons travel. So you really have to calculate a different "enough" each time you use atomic energy. Some of these "enoughs" are still military secrets. This amount is called the *critical mass*. Because when you have it, you have a little crisis on your hands.

If you have less than the critical mass, the neutrons that come shooting out of your first split nucleus may be wasted. Since atoms are

Why is there a "critical mass"?

mostly empty space, a neutron can go quite far, even through a heavy metal like uranium, before it bumps into a nucleus. And before it has a chance to do that, it might have shot right out of the lump. So if the lump is too small, so many neutrons are wasted that no chain reaction starts.

But if the lump is large enough, somewhere in it one of the billions and billions of atoms will split. It may split by itself, because uranium is radioactive. Or it may be split by one of the strange rays from outer space called *cosmic rays*. And when it splits, its neutrons will send the atomic blaze sweeping through the critical mass.

The simplest kind of atomic chain reaction is the one that

How does an A-bomb work? takes place in a bomb. In the bomb

are two or more lumps of isotope. Each lump weighs less than the critical mass, but together they weigh more than the critical mass. They are a safe distance apart. But back of these lumps are small lumps of ordinary explosive. At the right moment, these explosives are set off. They shoot the isotope lumps toward each other. The critical mass is formed. The atom bomb goes off.

First there is one fission. Then the two neutrons cause two fissions. Then each causes two, so there are four. Eight. Sixteen. Sixty-four. . . .

It does not sound fast. But it is surprising how fast the numbers grow when you keep multiplying by two! In the tenth "generation" of fissions, there would be 512. In the twentieth — 524,288. In the eightieth — more than 1,208,900,000,000,000,000,-000,000. And all this would happen in a fantastically small fraction of a second.

That is what happened at Hiroshima on August 6, 1945.

If atomic energy could be used only for blowing up people, not

How can we tame the A-bomb? many scientists would have worked on it. Even while the war

was going on, physicists and engineers were busy inventing machines which would keep chain reaction going, but going slowly, so the energy could be used to run electric generators, ships, and perhaps even airplanes. These machines are called *reactors*.

Three of the hardest problems these scientists had to solve were: Getting enough neutrons. Not getting too many neutrons. Making the neutrons go at the right speed.

They got enough neutrons because the right isotopes had to be manufactured to use in the war.

They had to learn how to keep the chain reaction from building up with an explosion — 2, 4, 8 and *out!* It is one thing to drench your U-235 or plutonium with flying neutrons in a bomb you have dropped on your enemy. It is another thing to do it when you are anywhere around. In order to run a reactor, you have to have just the right number of neutrons — not too many, not too few. And you cannot learn to do this by trial and error, because you can only make *one* atomic error.

is the Armour research
...tor in Chicago, Illinois.

How do we keep from getting too many neutrons? Many substances are thirsty for neutrons. They soak them up as a blotter soaks up water. This means that all the things with which you build a reactor must be very pure, so that you do not waste neutrons. But it also means that you can put safety-controls in your reactor. In Professor Fermi's first working reactor on the squash court at Stagg Field, he put rods of cadmium, a neutron-thirsty metal. A hasty movement of an inch too much in putting out a rod might have meant disaster. He had three men ready with pails of cadmium stuff just in case. Now we know a lot more about how reactors will react, and we have learned how to make them safe.

And the scientists learned to control the speed of neutrons. This was important because, for most of the reactors we have invented so far, slow-moving neutrons are better than fast-moving neutrons. That sounds strange.

Why are slow neutrons better than fast neutrons? But suppose you are sitting with your family in a restaurant. You have been sitting there for twenty minutes and no one has taken your order or even brought the rolls, and you are all fidgety. Waiters are going past, carrying food to other tables. The whole family is trying to attract their attention. Two waiters pass. One is rushing along with a tray of empty dishes. The other has just made out somebody's bill and is walking slowly. Which do you think you can get to stop at your table?

And the problem is more complicated than that. Suppose someone at the next table was also trying to call a waiter. And suppose he was very good at it, especially at tripping up fast-moving waiters. The only waiter you would ever catch would be a slow waiter. Unless you have pure U-235 in your reactor,

43

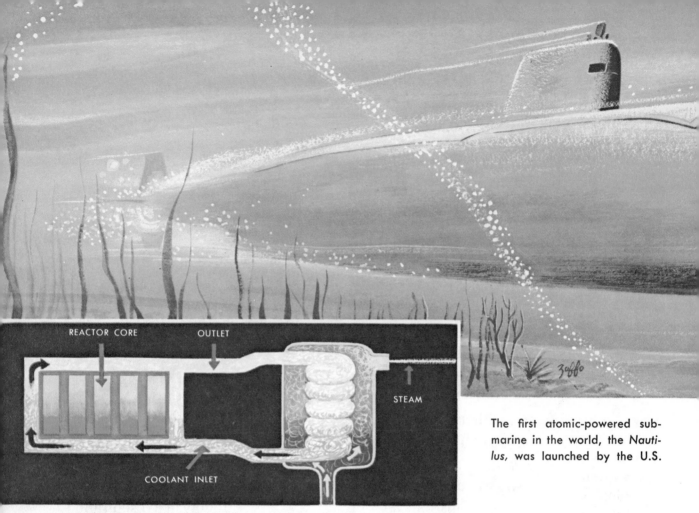

REACTOR CORE OUTLET

STEAM

COOLANT INLET

The first atomic-powered submarine in the world, the *Nautilus*, was launched by the U.S.

you must slow down your neutrons. Because if there is any U-238, it will grab the fast neutrons and not *split*. The only neutrons the U-235 could get would be the slow ones.

Many things slow down neutrons. But you have to pick things that will not absorb them. One of the first and best is carbon. Professor Fermi chose carbon, in the form of graphite, to put between the little lumps of uranium in the Stagg Field reactor.

Another slower-down of neutrons is water. Water is easy to handle, and it is especially useful because it boils. If the chain reaction starts to get out of hand and the reactor gets too hot,

How do we make the neutrons slow down?

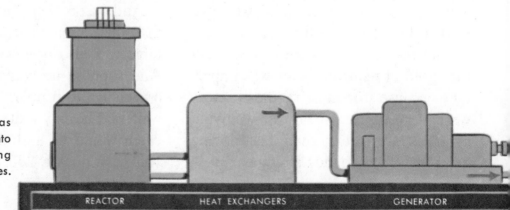

Atomic energy has been transformed into electricity, supplying power to communities.

REACTOR   HEAT EXCHANGERS   GENERATOR

44

the water will boil away, the neutrons will speed up and miss the nuclei, and the chain reaction will die down. The trouble is, water is made of hydrogen and oxygen atoms, and ordinary hydrogen is very greedy for neutrons. *Heavy hydrogen*, the second isotope, is not; and *heavy water*, made with this isotope, is used a lot as a moderator. But it is rare and expensive, so we have been learning how to use ordinary water.

A substance used to slow down neutrons is called a *moderator*. The first thing to do in designing a reactor is to choose the moderator. We talk about

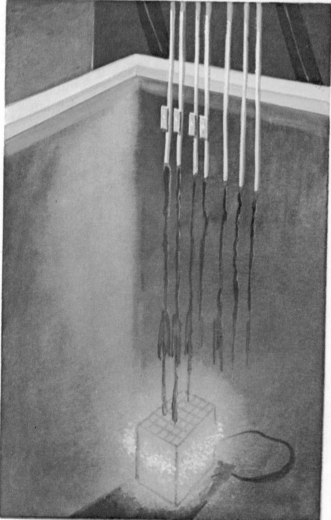

In an atomic "swimming pool" reactor, moderated by water, the nuclear radiation causes a blue glow.

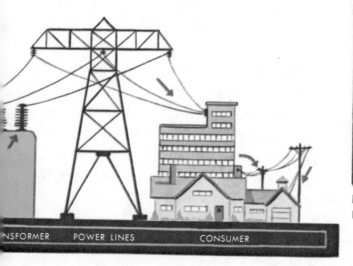

reactors as being *water moderated, graphite moderated* and so on.

Engineers and physicists have now invented dozens of dif-

What kinds of jobs can reactors do?

ferent kinds of reactors to do different things. But all reactors can: (1) produce a great quantity of heat and (2) bombard things with different kinds of atomic particles.

Power reactors are furnaces. They heat water or some other

How do we use reactors?

stuff that boils, and drive engines. We have a whole fleet of submarines whose engines run by atomic heat. Surface vessels also are run by atomic energy. The United States has an atomic-powered steamship, the *U.S.S. Savannah*, and the Soviet Union has built an atom-powered icebreaker, the *Lenin*.

So far, we have not been able to use atomic reactors to power automobiles and airplanes, because atomic power plants are too heavy. Their weight is due mainly to the thick metal shielding needed to prevent stray atomic particles and rays from burning or poisoning passengers. In 1970, however, the United States successfully tested an atomic rocket engine for propelling spacecraft.

When shielding is not needed, small atomic power reactors have been used very successfully. The *Apollo 11* astronauts, on the surface of the moon, set up a small reactor that uses plutonium-238 to provide power for a seismometer (a device for measuring moonquakes) that broadcasts its readings back to

Earth. *Apollo 12* set up a small SNAP (*S*ystems for *N*uclear *A*uxiliary *P*ower) reactor to provide power for scientific instruments left behind on the moon.

At the beginning of 1971, there were 111 atomic power reactors in fifteen countries. Those in the United States produce almost exactly as much atomic energy as reactors in all of the other countries combined. Most of the reactors in the United States are within huge electric generating plants where they heat large quantities of water to form steam. The steam powers turbines, which in turn run electric generators that produce vast amounts of electricity for lighting, heating, and running appliances in homes and for running machinery in factories.

A very important type of reactor is the *breeder*, which not only produces power, but at the same time makes more atomic fuel (mainly plutonium) than it uses. This reactor pays its own costs.

Reactors can be used to make radioactive isotopes of

How do we use new isotopes?

ordinary elements. These are very useful to research scientists. For instance, suppose you are a doctor who wants to know if medicine designed to cure disease in a particular part of the body actually goes to that part of a patient's body. You add a very small amount of a radioactive isotope to the medicine. The radioactive atoms of the isotope act as labels attached to the molecules of the medicine. The radioactivity can be traced, by an instrument called a *Geiger counter*, as it circulates throughout the patient's body.

Suns Made to Order

Where do stars get their energy?

We know that the sun — like all stars — makes atomic energy. This energy is not made by fission, but by *fusion*. The sun combines two atoms of hydrogen, making helium. Our binding energy chart (page 30) tells us that an enormous amount of mass — atomically speaking — is converted into energy when this happens.

How does the sun combine these atoms?

What happens inside the sun?

It is so big that its gravity, pulling everything toward the center of its huge mass, creates an unbelievable pressure there. The matter at the sun's center is stripped-down hydrogen — just nuclei, because there is no room for the outer electrons. The inside of the sun is very hot — about 20 million degrees Celsius. Under these conditions, protons turn to neutrons, shoving out electrons. Proton-neutron pairs — which are the nuclei of heavy hydrogen — are forced together to become helium. This probably happens in many ways, but all of them give off vast amounts of energy.

It takes a little over eight minutes for that energy to travel to the earth, once it works its way to the surface of the sun. But it takes 10,000 years for the energy to work its way from the center of the sun to the surface.

How does an H-bomb work?

When the trial atom bomb exploded at Alamogordo on July 16, 1945, scientists realized that they could not only make fission-energy, they could now make fusion-energy the way the sun does. For at the heart of Fat Man, there were millions of degrees of temperature, just as there are at the heart of the sun. And there were millions of pounds of pressure. If we were to put the right kind of hydrogen atoms into the heart of an atomic explosion, we could make a second explosion of energy that would make Fat Man look scrawny.

The right kind of hydrogen is the heaviest of the three hydrogen isotopes, tritium, a radioactive atom with one proton and two neutrons in its nucleus. By crushing a tritium nucleus with another tritium nucleus, we get helium and two neutrons and 11 million electron volts. By crushing a tritium nucleus into a "heavy hydrogen" nucleus, we get helium, one neutron, and 17 million electron volts.

Fission: When an atomic nucleus splits. *Fusion*: Two lightweight atomic nuclei join, forming a heavier nucleus.

NUCLEAR FISSION

NUCLEAR FUSION

Although the H-bomb that exploded on Eniwetok Atoll in the Pacific on November 1, 1952 — and not only melted a whole island but boiled it away — is hidden in military secrecy, we know now that *there is no limit to the energy we can make from the atom.*

The trouble is, we have found no way

Can we tame the H-bomb?

to control this terrible and wonderful new force. We can make the pressures and temperatures we need — for an instant. But if we want to make fusion energy steadily, as the sun does, we must have a container that will hold those pressures and those temperatures. What can hold them?

We have tried magnetic bottles, in which gases are trapped and squeezed without ever touching solid matter. At first, this method showed promise, but it could not quite be made to work. It was abandoned, and with no other way in sight, the problem of controlling an atomic-fusion reaction did not appear to have a solution. Then, in the early 1970's, Soviet physicists were able to create a magnetic bottle that held a fusion reaction for a few thousandths of a second. American physicists, using the same method, also got good results. Now there is new hope that atomic-fusion reactions can be tamed and made usable for mankind's needs for power.

The earth is running out of water for

How can we make fresh water out of ocean water?

people to use for drinking, bathing, cooking, and for other purposes that require fresh — not salt

—water. Rivers, streams and lakes cannot provide enough fresh water. The only source we can look to now is the ocean. But ocean water is salt water, so we must get the salt out of the ocean water, a process called desalination.

One way to get the salt out of sea water is to boil it. This changes the water to steam. Then we cool the steam, and this changes the steam back to water — fresh water. The steam leaves the salt behind, and the water from the steam is fresh. The only trouble with this process is that the heat required to boil the sea water must come from fuels such as coal, coke or oil. These fuels are expensive, and so then is fresh water.

However, if we use atomic energy as fuel in an atomic reactor, we can get very much heat for a very long time fairly cheaply (after the cost of the reactor). In fact, if we use breeder reactors, we not only get heat, but the reactor makes more fuel, paying its operating costs. One of the peacetime uses for atomic energy is in desalination.

Producing atomic energy, like many

Do reactors pollute the environment?

other industrial processes, contributes to pollution of the environment. Radioactive gases and solid wastes from reactors must be disposed of without contaminating the atmosphere, the rivers, and the soil with deadly radioactive particles. Reactors are cooled by water from rivers. The hot water discharged into rivers may kill fish and plants. And so, controlling atomic-reactor pollution becomes an important challenge of the Atomic Age.